THIS BOOK makes a bid to
ing has in modern life. In
styles of ambitious young pe
entertaining can bring small islands of peace, friendship and beauty. In our otherwise stressful lives, this art can bring opportunities to create beauty and elegance.

Says Vimla Patil, "Since I believe that the creation of beauty and elegance, warmth and sharing is the basic purpose of all life, I am proud to present this collection of recipes divided into convenient menus for seasons, festivals, family and social occasions and for the promotion of business."

Vimla Patil is undoubtedly one of the most widely known women journalists and social workers of India. Editor of *Femina*, India's most widely read and popular women's magazine, she has authored several books and directs a professional team of models, fashion experts, choreographers, stage and prop creators to produce India's finest textile promotions.

THIS BOOK makes a bid to recognize the place entertaining has in modern life. In the frenetic, fast-forward life-styles of ambitious young people, well-planned and relaxed entertaining can bring small islands of peace, friendship and beauty. In our otherwise stressful lives, this act can bring opportunities to create beauty and elegance.

Says Vimla Patil: "Since I believe that the creation of beauty and elegance, warmth and sharing is the basic purpose of all life, I am proud to present this collection of recipes divided into convenient menus for seasons, festivals, family and social occasions and for the promotion of business."

Vimla Patil is undoubtedly one of the most widely known women journalists and social workers of India. Editor of *Femina*, India's most widely read and popular women's magazine, she has authored several books and directs a professional team of models, fashion experts, choreographers, stage and prop creators to produce India's finest textile promotions.

Entertaining Indian Style

recipes for all occasions

VIMLA PATIL

UBSPD

UBS Publishers' Distributors Ltd.

New Delhi • Bombay • Bangalore • Madras
• Calcutta • Patna • Kanpur • London

UBS Publishers' Distributors Ltd.
5 Ansari Road, New Delhi 110 002.
Bombay, Bangalore, Madras,
Calcutta, Patna, Kanpur, London.

First Published 1992
First Reprint 1993

ISBN 81-85674-16-7

Cover Design: UBS Art Studio
Cover Photo : Sondeep Shankar

Lasertypeset at Rajkamal Electric Press

Printed at NU TECH PHOTOLITHOGRAPHERS SHAHDARA DELHI-110 095

Preface

Sharing food with family and friends is an age-old tradition in India. Every festival, every family function, even the arrival of a new season is considered an occasion for merry-making. An important part of the joy of such celebrations is the cooking of mouth-watering delicacies—both savoury and sweet.

Feasts of unbelievable grandeur and opulence are recorded in India's mythology and history and the country's heritage of centuries reveals that entertaining guests has been the pride of every home—rich or poor.

In the modern world, entertaining people at a feast has acquired subtler shades of meaning than just the sharing of food. Serving a fabulous meal in a beautiful environment gives the host and hostess an opportunity to express their aesthetic abilities. Because of the internationalisation of food cultures today, table arts include Japanese flower arrangements, Thai vegetable-carving crafts, Czech crystal, English bone china, Chinese motifed crockery, Irish linen, German cutlery and of course the unfathomable wealth of India's own ethnic pots and basketry, painted lacquerwork and textiles of exotic variety to decorate a table for serving an exquisite meal. The preparation of the meal itself is an exercise in imaginative planning. In deciding upon the menu, the hosts can consider not only the traditional dinner or lunch but also plan an elaborate breakfast, a cool and invigorating salad spread, a really rich high tea, a hodge-podge of fast foods or even a decorative pot luck.

Added to this is the surfeit of seasonal entertaining, or festive occasions or simply the warm and cosy atmosphere of women getting together for a happy function. The more people-oriented our business and social life has become, the more acute is the need for enhancing the art of being delightful hosts.

This book makes a bid to recognize the place entertaining has achieved in modern life. In the frenzied, fast-forward lifestyles of ambitious young people, well-planned and relaxed entertaining can bring small islands of peace, friendship and beauty.

Since I believe that the creation of beauty and elegance, warmth and sharing is the basic purpose of all life, I am proud to present this collection of recipes divided into convenient menus for seasons, festivals, family and social occasions and for the promotion of business.

I would like to thank Bharat Chanda, S.N. Kulkarni, Pankaj Liya, Mukesh Munim and Varsha Tambe for the photographs in this book. My thanks are also to Aneeta Pillay, Shubhada Karkare, Ranjana Thatte, Ms. Phanase, Megha Hardikar, Berel Patrao and Ms. Saptarshi for providing the locations for photography sessions.

BOMBAY VIMLA PATIL

Contents

seasonal entertainment

VASANT RITU

(A Spring-Time Feast)

The artistic soul of India is bound by imperceptible gossamer-fine silken threads with the season of *Vasant* or spring. For thousands of years, this season has been celebrated in romantic prose, poetry, music, dance and folklore by great artists. Indeed, in the *Bhagvad Gita* the beautiful Krishna himself says that among the seasons, he represents spring-time and one of his names, i.e. *Madhav*, is a derivative of *Madhavi*, a Sanskrit name for the season of spring.

In the sub-continent of India, springtime signals the call of the *Koel* or the cuckoo. He sings at sunrise and sunset, as if celebrating the mild golden sunshine of the warm days of this season. His piercing, musical trills are enigmatic, for few can spot him, hidden among the newly verdant clumps of trees.

Spring is also the season of fruits, flowers and mango blossoms whose fragrance softly pervades the mellow air. *Vasant* is a season of good eating. Outdoor dinners served in flowering bowers in pastel shaded ambience or lazy afternoon lunches served in sun-kissed colour schemes are beautiful and memorable. The menus planned for symbolising this colourful season also use romantic ingredients like saffron, dry fruits, luscious fruits and a large number of creative dishes in celebration of this season of the reawakening of life and the rejuvenation of energy!

menu

kali mirchwala kesri murgh
mewawala gosht lazeez
alu matki usal
khatti bharwan bhindi
dal sartaaj
tarkewala mirch achar
paneer aam ka pudding
kharbuja papite ka salad

KALI MIRCHWALA KESRI MURGH

(Saffron-Flavoured Peppery Chicken)

Serves: 6 **Cooking Time: 1 hr 30 mins**

1 kg. chicken, skinned,cut into cubes, deboned
2 cups yoghurt, beaten
1 tbsp. pepper powder
5 onions,grated
2 tbsp. garam masala
1 tbsp. red chilli powder
1 tsp. turmeric powder
1 tbsp.ginger-garlic paste
$^1/_4$ tsp. saffron
$^1/_2$ cup top of milk
2 bay leaves
2 tbsp. coriander leaves, chopped
Oil as needed
Salt to taste

Mix chicken with yoghurt, salt, ginger–garlic paste and all powdered masalas. Reserve for 30 minutes. Heat 5 tbsp. oil in a pressure cooker. Add bay leaves and onion. Brown. Add chicken with spices and yoghurt and stir fry.

Add 2 cups water and pressure-cook till done. Remove to a servingdish. Cover with saffron soaked in top of milk. Sprinkle coriander leaves and serve with *parathas.*

MEWAWALA GOSHT LAZEEZ

(Meat with Dry Fruit)

Serves: 6 **Cooking Time: 1 hr 30 mins**

1 kg. mutton leg, boneless, flattened by a mallet
1 cup cherries, chopped fine
1 cup mixed nuts, raisins, chopped fine
5 eggs, hardboiled, shelled chopped finely
$1^1/_2$ cups tomato puree
1 cup green peas, cooked
4 onions, sliced, ground
1 tbsp. ginger-garlic paste
1 tbsp. garam masala powder
1 tbsp. chilli powder
2 cups yoghurt
1 cup coriander leaves, chopped
$^1/_2$ cup oil
Salt and sugar to taste

Mix nuts, cherries, raisins, eggs, coriander leaves and salt and put in the centre of the meat. Roll tightly and secure with thread. Wrap in greased greaseproof paper and steam in a pressure cooker till meat is tender. Remove and arrange in a serving dish.

Heat oil. Add onion, ginger-garlic paste. Brown. Add tomato and yoghurt. Cook till oil separates. Add chilli powder, peas, garam masala and sugar and salt to taste. Pour this sauce over the meat, placing it in a pan of water heat in an oven till top is browned and gravy is thick. Garnish with coriander leaves over and serve with *parathas.*

ALU MATKI USAL

(Potatoes with Sprouted Beans)

Serves: 6 **Cooking Time: 1 hr**

1 cup *matki* beans
3 potatoes, peeled, cut into slices
4 curry leaves
1 tsp. turmeric powder
1 tsp. garam masala powder
2 tsp. chilli powder
1 tsp. sugar
1 tsp. cumin seeds
2 tbsp. fresh coconut, grated
$^1/_2$ cup coriander leaves,chopped
1 onion, chopped
Oil as needed
Salt to taste

Sprout matki beans as follows:

Soak in water overnight after cleaning. Drain away all water in the morning and tie in a piece of muslin. Hang for eight hours. Wash and make ready for use.

Cook beans in water or pressure steam till just soft but whole. Drain and reserve.

Heat oil and deep-fry slices of potatoes. Put on absorbent paper. Sprinkle with salt Reserve all oil except 3 tbsp. Add cumin seeds and curry leaves. Then add onions and fry till golden. Add beans and all powdered spices, salt and sugar. Mix well. Put in a serving dish and cover with slices of fried potatoes. Garnish with coconut and coriander leaves. Serve hot with rice.

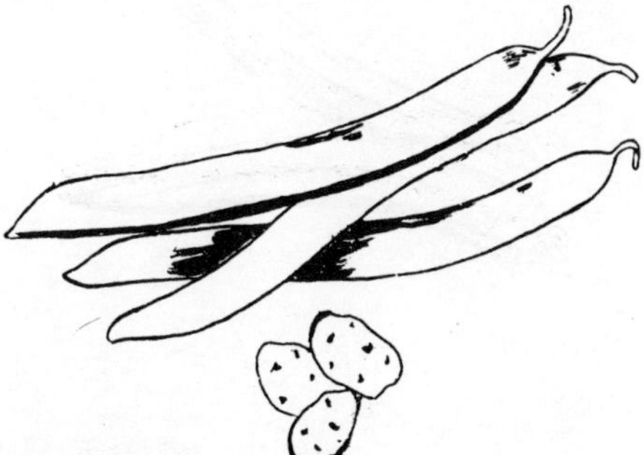

KHATTI BHARWAN BHINDI

(Stuffed Lady Fingers)

Serves: 6 **Cooking Time: 45 mins**

$^{3}/_{4}$ kg. tender lady fingers
3 tbsp. mango powder (*amchur*)
3 tbsp. cumin seed powder
1 tsp. chilli powder
$^{1}/_{2}$ tsp. turmeric powder
3 tbsp. fresh coconut,grated
$^{1}/_{2}$ cup coriander leaves, chopped
1 tsp. caramelized sugar
4 tbsp. oil
Salt to taste

Wipe the lady fingers clean. Remove stems and tips and slit lengthwise. Mix all powdered spices, sugar, coconut, coriander leaves and salt. Stuff the lady fingers with this mixture. Heat oil in a non-stick pan and arrange the stuffed *bhindis* in it. Do not cover. Cook on a low flame, turning occasionally without burning or breaking the vegetable. Serve with *parathas.*

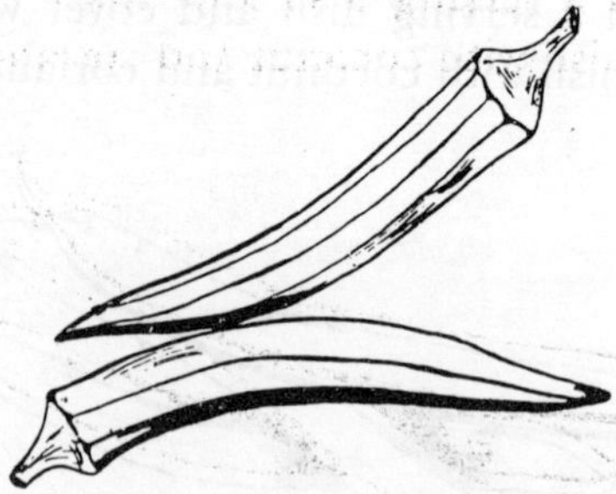

DAL SARTAAJ

(Lentils With Spices)

Serves: 6 **Cooking Time: 45 mins**

1 cup *tuvar* dal (red gram *dal*)
1 tsp. green chilli paste
$^1/_2$ tsp. turmeric powder
$^1/_2$ cup cooked green peas
2 tomatoes, chopped
5 curry leaves
2 cloves garlic, chopped
2 red chillies
2 tbsp. oil
2 tbsp. fresh coconut, grated
2 tbsp. coriander leaves
1 tsp. mustard seeds
Salt to taste

Boil *dal* in a pressure cooker. Remove. Churn lightly. Add chilli paste, peas, tomatoes, curry leaves, coconut, turmeric powder and salt.

Boil once. Heat oil. Add mustard seeds, red chillies and garlic. Brown and pour over *dal*. Serve with rice.

TARKEWALA MIRCH ACHAR

(Green Chilli Pickle)

Serves: 6 **Cooking Time: 30 mins**

250 gm. long green chillies, cut into pieces
$^1/_4$ cup sesame seeds
$^1/_2$ cup mustard seeds
$^1/_2$ tsp. fenugreek seeds
$^1/_2$ tsp. turmeric powder
2 tbsp. oil
$^1/_4$ tsp. asafoetida
1 tbsp. lemon juice
Salt to taste

Heat $^1/_2$ tsp. oil and stir fry mustard seeds (Reserve a pinch). Remove. Stir fry sesame seeds. Remove. Stir fry fenugreek seeds and asafoetida. Remove. Grind all these to a rough powder. Heat remaining oil. Add the pinch of mustard seeds and a pinch of asafoetida. Add chilli pieces, turmeric powder and salt. Cook for a few minutes and add powdered spices. Cook covered for 10 minutes. Remove and add lemon juice. Cool and bottle. It can be used for a week if refrigerated.

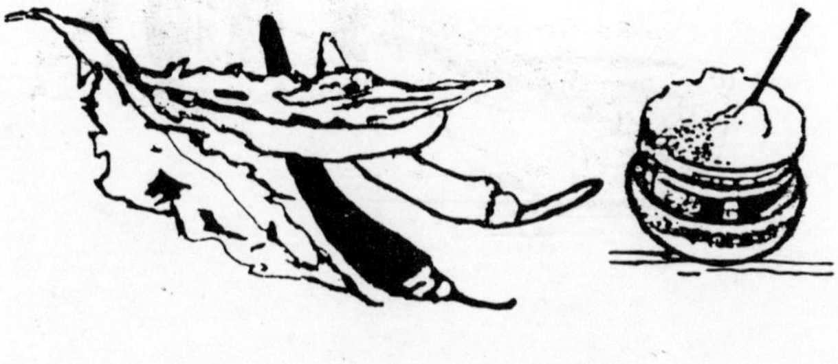

PANEER AAM KA PUDDING

(Mango Cream Pie)

Serves: 6 **Cooking Time: 2 hrs**

2 cups crunchy cookies
1 cup crushed almonds or cashewnuts
$^{3}/_{4}$ cup butter
2 cups *paneer*, ground to a paste
$^{3}/_{4}$ cup ground sugar
2 cups mango pulp
2 tinned mango pieces, sliced
2 tbsp. gelatine, softened in
$^{1}/_{2}$ cup hot water
2 tbsp. whipped cream

Mix crunchy cookies, nut powder and butter well. Line a pie dish and freeze till set.

Mix *paneer*, mango pulp and sugar in a liquidizer. Remove. Add cream and cooled gelatine. Stir well and add a few mango slices. Put in the set pie crust and decorate with slices of mango and whipped cream. Freeze till set. Turn out on a platter to serve.

• • •

KHARBUJA PAPITE KA SALAD

(Melon Papaya Salad)

Serves: 6 **Cooking Time: 45 mins**

$^{1}/_{2}$ watermelon
$^{1}/_{2}$ honeydew melon
1 small papaya
$^{1}/_{2}$ cup, lemon juice
$^{1}/_{2}$ tsp. pepper powder
2 sprigs of mint
Salt and sugar to taste

Using a scoop, cut out tiny balls from all the fruits. Arrange in a bowl and sprinkle with lemon juice, salt and sugar. Decorate with mint and chill before serving.

seasonal entertainment

GRISHMA RITU

(Summer Bounty)

When the sun's orb burns with orange and gold intensity, the mountains and plains of India lie spread-eagled in a somnolent stupor. The parched brown valleys of the Ganga heartland crack with their thirst for rain and the subcontinent sizzles under the red haze of the summer heat.

But summer also ushers in a procession of vegetables grown in irrigated farms. Tender corn cobs, vegetables and melons of many varieties are specialities of the hot months. Almost all over India farms grow corn cobs, these days, including baby corns. All root vegetables too are available in summer months. Summer is a season of outdoor or *patio* eating, when evenings bring relief from the scorching heat of the sun. Cool, minty salads, simple innovative *barbecued* or baked dishes and basic rice can make an excellent menu for such entertaining. Summer evenings are occasions for laid back elegance, for white linen and lace, for *mogra* flowers spreading their light, heady fragrance from the cascade of flowers on the dining table.

menu

mewawala tandoor guchchi murgh
moongphali ke chawal
kathal ki tikia
chukandar kali mirch ka salad
faras bean pudina dahiwale
aloo narielka meetha
aam ka pudding

MEWAWALA TANDOOR GUCHCHI MURGH

(Oven-Cooked Chicken with Mushrooms and Raisins)

Serves: 6 **Cooking Time: 1 hr 30 mins**

12 chicken legs, skinned
2 tbsp. chilli powder
2 tbsp. garam masala powder *or tandoori* masala powder
1 tbsp. ginger-garlic paste
1 cup yoghurt
24 large mushrooms
$^1/_2$ cup cashewnuts/raisins
2 green chillies, chopped
5 tbsp. oil
Salt to taste

Marinate chicken in powdered masalas and ginger-garlic paste mixed with yoghurt and salt. Put in nuts and raisins and mushrooms. In a baking dish lined with foil, arrange chicken, mushrooms and nuts etc. Pour remaining sauce and oil over. Cover with foil and bake till done. Before serving, remove top foil and grill for a few minutes. Serve garnished with chopped chillies.

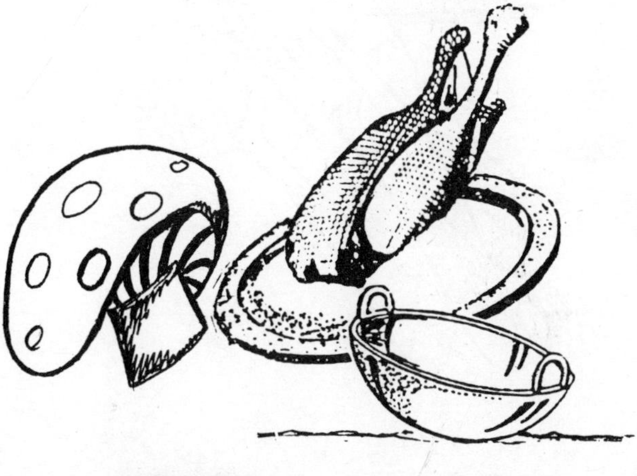

MOONGPHALI KE CHAWAL

(Peanut Rice)

Serves: 6 **Cooking Time: 1 hr**

1/2 cup peanuts, soaked in water, boiled
1 cup rice, cooked
1 tbsp. tamarind paste
1 onion, chopped
1 tbsp. garam masala powder
1 tsp. chilli powder
1 tsp. sesame seeds
1/2 tsp. mustard seeds
3 tbsp. oil
1 cup coconut, grated
Salt to taste

Heat a pan. Add sesame seeds. When they pop, add oil. Add mustard seeds. Add onions. Brown. Add tamarind paste and powdered spices. Add peanuts, rice and salt to taste. Stir till blended and heat through. Serve hot.

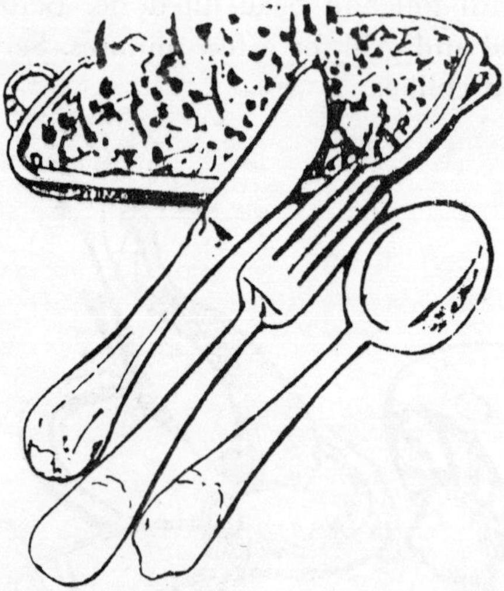

KATHAL KI TIKIA

(Jackfruit Cutlets)

Serves: 6 **Cooking Time: 1 hr 15 mins**

1/2 kg. jackfruit, chopped, boiled
3 medium sized potatoes, boiled
1 tbsp. gram flour
2 slices bread
1 big onion, chopped
1/2 tsp.chilli powder
1/2 tsp. cumin powder
1/2 tsp. coriander powder
1/4 tsp. turmeric powder
1/2 tsp. ginger-garlic paste
2 tsp. tomato sauce
1/2 tbsp. coriander leaves. chopped
1/4 cup arrowroot powder
1 cup crumbs
Oil
Salt to taste

Dissolve arrowroot in a little water. Mix without lumps and keep aside. Soak the bread slices in water. Squeeze out the water. Mix the jackfruit pieces,potatoes, gram flour and all the other ingredients except crumbs. Mash and mix well. Knead into a dough.

Heat one tbsp. oil and stir fry the dough. Shape into small balls and flatten each ball slightly. Dip in arrowroot batter and coat with crumbs. Press to make sure that the cutlets are well coated. Deep fry in hot oil to a golden brown. Serve hot with sauce or tamarind chutney.

CHUKANDAR KALI MIRCH KA SALAD

(Beet Salad with Pepper)

Serves: 6 **Cooking Time: 30 mins**

3 beetroots, boiled,peeled, cut into strips
4 spring onions, cut into strips
2 capsicums, cut into strips
$^1/_4$ cup oil
$^1/_4$ cup white vinegar
1 tbsp. mustard paste
1 tsp. pepper powder
1 tbsp. caramelized sugar
Salt to taste

Mix all vegetables and put in a salad bowl. Mix vinegar, oil, mustard, pepper, sugar and salt and toss into salad. Chill before serving.

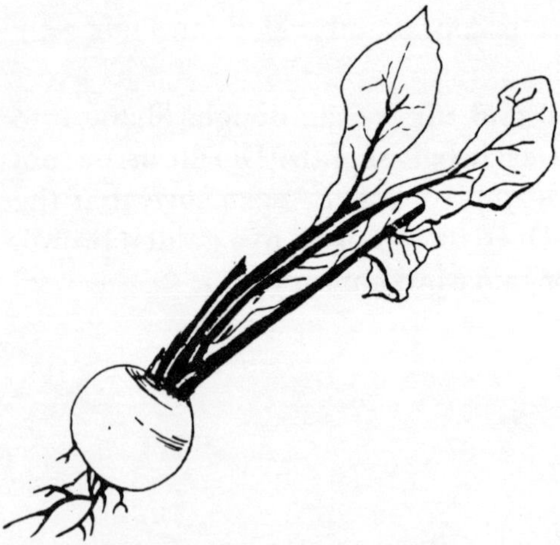

FARAS BEAN PUDINA DAHIWALE

(French Beans in Spiced Yoghurt)

Serves: 6 **Cooking Time: 45 mins**

400 gm. French beans, threads removed, cut into strips, cooked to crunchy stage
4 capsicums, cut into strips
2 onions chopped finely
2 tbsp. oil
$^{1}/_{2}$ tsp. garlic paste
1 tbsp. lemon juice
$^{1}/_{2}$ tsp. sugar
Salt to taste

For Sauce:
1 cup yoghurt
2 tbsp. cream
2 tbsp.mint leaves, chopped
2 tbsp. coriander leaves, chopped
$^{1}/_{2}$ tsp. chilli powder
$^{1}/_{2}$ tsp. pepper powder
1 tsp. caramel syrup
Salt to taste

Mix beans, capsicums and onions with oil, lemon juice, sugar, garlic paste and salt. Toss and chill.

Blend all sauce ingredients and chill. Before serving, pour sauce over vegetables in a suitable pattern and serve chilled.

ALOO NARIELKA MEETHA

(Potato Fudge)

Serves: 6 **Cooking Time: 1 hr 30 mins**

- 5 large potatoes,boiled, peeled, ground to a paste
- 1 coconut, grated, ground coarsely
- $1^1/_4$ kg. sugar
- 1 cup cream
- 1 tsp.cardamom powder
- 6 tbsp. ghee
- 2 tbsp. castor sugar

Mix potato paste, coconut, sugar and cream. Heat 3 tbsp. ghee in a pan and add the above mixture. Stir fry till pink, adding castor sugar, cardamom powder and all the remaining ghee except 1 teaspoon. When the mixture becomes a ball, remove and pat into a ghee-greased platter. Cool and cut into diamond shapes with a greased knife. Serve on a bed of rose petals.

AAM KA PUDDING

(Mango Cream Treat)

Serves: 6

Cooking Time: 30 mins

$1^1/_4$ kg. sponge cake
4 large ripe mangoes (or tinned) peeled, cubed
$1^1/_2$ cups thick cream, beaten
Vanilla essence
12 cherries

Cut sponge into fingers and arrange in a dish. Wet with the leftover mango juice taken from skins squeezed in water. Mix a drop of vanilla essence in $^1/_4$ cup water and sprinkle over cake. Reserve. After 15 minutes, cover cake with mango cubes and pour cream over to cover. Chop cherries and decorate the top. Chill and serve cold.

seasonal entertainment

VARSHA RITU

(Monsoon Medley)

Tropical countries are considered mysterious and romantic because of their deep, thick and inscrutable rain forests. Huge banians, peepals, deodars, cockscombs, silk cotton and other trees grow skywards in these forests creating a thick green canopy and the silky silence rings, permeating the darkness. The patter of monsoon rain turns the forests into magical paradises where globules of prismatic water glint from green leaves.

There is a special beauty and a deep emotional significance to the rainy season in India. All the romantic folklore extols its abundant beauty because an agricultural society regards and reveres monsoons as the life-giving source.

Not surprisingly, the *Varsha Ritu* or the monsoon season is symbolic of abundance. Nearly all of India's festivals come in this season and thousands of special dishes are cooked to celebrate these festivals in various parts of India.

Monsoons are a cosy season for entertaining. After a shower has washed the landscape and a moist silence steals into the twinkling night, it is time to get together for a hot, many splendoured meal featuring the produce of the season.

menu

chowkone puris
bhutte ke pancake
hare pyaz aur bhutte ka shorba
parchedar sayel gosht
matarwale sunhare chawal
double roti ke taco
baingan tandoori cheesewale
sharife ki rabdi

CHOWKONE PURIS

(Four-Cornered Puris)

Serves: 6 **Cooking Time: 1 hr**

3 cup wholemeal flour
1 tbsp. ghee
Salt to taste
Oil for frying

Mix flour, ghee, salt and enough water to make a stiff dough. Make small balls and roll out into round *puris.* Fold from four sides to make a square. Roll just once and fry in hot oil till golden. Fry in batches and serve hot.

• •

BHUTTE KE PANCAKE

(Corn Pancakes)

Serves: 6 **Cooking Time : 1 hr**

3 corn cobs
1 cup flour
1 egg, beaten
2 green chillies,minced
2 tbsp.coriander leaves,
Oil for frying
Salt to taste

Remove corn kernels and cook till soft. Mash well. Make a batter with the flour, egg and water. Add corn, chillies, coriander leaves and salt.

Heat a non-stick griddle and grease it. Pour spoonfuls of batter and shallow fry pancakes on both sides till golden. Serve hot with any chutney.

HARE PYAZ AUR BHUTTE KA SHORBA

(Corn and Onion Broth)

Serves: 6 **Cooking Time: 45 mins**

3 spring onions, chopped
1 carrot, grated
1 capsicum, chopped
1 tomato, chopped
$^{1}/_{2}$ tsp. garlic paste
2 tbsp. flour (*maida*), roasted in a little butter
3 cups milk and water mixed half and half
2 tbsp. butter
1 cup corn, cooked
$^{1}/_{2}$ tsp. chilli powder
1 tbsp. cream
Salt and pepper to taste

Heat butter in a pressure cooker. Add garlic, onions, carrots and capsicums. Cook till transluscent. Add tomatoes and corn. Mix flour with milk-water mixture leaving no lumps and add to vegetables Add salt and pepper and chilli powder. Cook covered for 10 minutes. When blended, serve topped with cream.

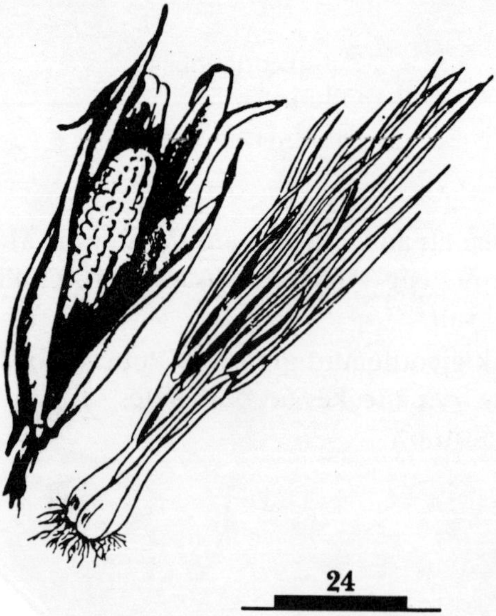

PARCHEDAR SAYEL GOSHT

(Mutton Curry)

Serves: 6 **Cooking Time: 1 hr 30 mins**

500 gm. mutton,cubed
3 onions, chopped
1 tbsp. garlic-ginger paste, mixed in one cup water
$1^1/_2$ tsp. chilli powder
1 tsp. green chilli paste
$^1/_2$ cup tomato *puree*
1 tbsp. coriander powder
$^1/_2$ tsp. turmeric powder
2 cups yoghurt
8 black peppercorns
8 cloves
1 tsp. cumin seeds
1 cup coriander leaves, chopped
$^1/_2$ cup oil
Salt to taste

Flatten meat cubes into *parchas* or flat pieces. Mix with yoghurt, salt, chilli, turmeric and coriander powders. Arrange half the onions in a pressure cooker at the bottom. Arrange the meat pieces with yoghurt sauce on top of the onions. Sprinkle ginger-garlic water over and add the rest of the onions with whole spices. Add two cups hot water and cook under pressure till done. Remove and cook till water content is reduced. Add oil and tomato *puree.* Stir cook till blended and oil separates. Add coriander leaves and serve hot.

MATARWALE SUNHARE CHAWAL

(Golden Pea Pulao)

Serves: 6 **Cooking Time: 1 hr**

$1^1/_2$ cup *basmati* rice, washed well
2 onions, chopped
1 tsp. sugar
1 cup tender peas
5 tbsp. oil
1 egg. hardboiled, shelled, sliced
Salt to taste

Heat sugar in a pressure cooker till it caramelizes. Add oil and heat. Add onions. Brown. Add rice and peas and stir fry till golden. Add salt and $3^1/_2$ cups hot water. Cook under pressure for 7 minutes. Cool and transfer to a serving dish. Decorate with egg slices.

• •

DOUBLE ROTI KE TACO

(Bread Tacos)

Serves: 6 **Cooking Time: 45 mins**

12 thin bread slices, trimmed
1 cup baked beans
1 cup mixed chopped onion, capsicum, cabbage, tomato
1 tsp. red chilli-garlic paste
$^1/_2$ tsp. green chilli-vinegar paste
1 tbsp. coriander leaves, chopped
Oil as needed
Salt and pepper to taste

Heat oil and fry all bread slices rolled around a tube so that they are shaped like *tacos.* Heat beans and season with salt and pepper. Fill each *taco* with beans, top with salad vegetables and sprinkle with both chilli pastes. Decorate with coriander leaves and serve while crunchy.

BAINGAN TANDOORI CHEESEWALE

(Baked Brinjals)

Serves: 6 **Cooking Time: 1 hr**

3 large, long brinjals
2 onions, grated
2 tomatoes, chopped
1 tsp. ginger-garlic paste
1 tsp. green chilli paste
1/2 tsp. chilli powder
1/2 tsp. lemon juice
3 tbsp. rice, cooked
3 tbsp. oil
Grated cheese as needed
Salt and pepper to taste

Remove stems and cut brinjals into two—from top to bottom. Scoop out flesh and apply lemon juice to brinjal cavities. Meanwhile heat oil. Add ginger-garlic and onions. Brown. Add tomatoes, brinjal flesh, green chilli paste, chilli powder and salt and pepper. Cook till soft and add rice and a little cheese. Spoon mixture into six greased brinjal cases and top with plenty of cheese. Bake in a hot oven till cases are soft and cheese has melted. Serve hot.

SHARIFE KI RABDI

(Custard Apple Sweet)

Serves: 6 **Cooking Time: 1 hr**

2 litres milk
1 small tin sweet condensed milk
1 cup *khoya*, unsweetened
3 custard apples, seeded
Sugar if needed
3 drops of vanilla essence

Boil milk gently till creamy. Remove cream. To the cooled milk, add condensed milk, broken *khoya* and essence. Blend completely and chill till thick. Just before serving, add the pulp of the custard apples so that the flavour is fresh. Serve very cold.

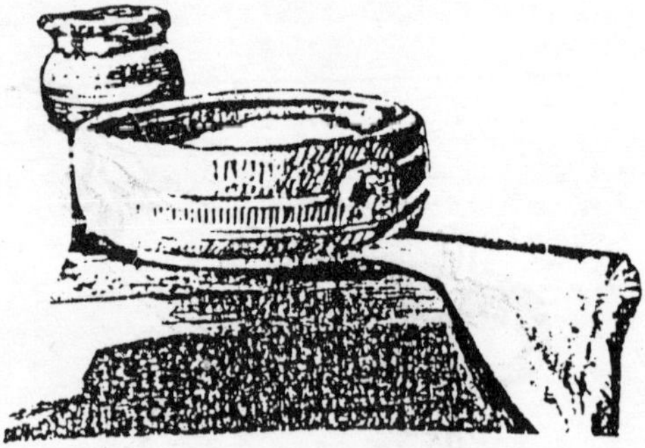

seasonal entertainment

SHARAD RITU

(Moonlit Majesty)

The nights of *Sharad Ritu*—the season which comes as a preamble to the shivering winter—are a delight. The moon shines bright and beautiful among the myriad stars in a deep blue sky, clear of the last monsoon clouds and the verdure spread by the monsoon over hills and valleys has not yet turned completely brown. *Sharad* is a time when outdoor eating—gatherings on terraces for song and dance on full moon nights is the order of the day. In fact, *Sharad Poornima* or the *Kojagiri* as the full moon day is called, is celebrated by distributing flavoured milk, enriched with pistachios and saffron and cooled under the moonlit sky.

It is also a season of plenty. The new harvests are in. The dry fruit market is full of goodies and lush winter vegetables beckon invitingly. It's indeed a season of happy entertaining.

menu

murgh jardaloowala
jhinga raiwala
dalka osaman
garam masale ka pizza
chawal kajudar
falon ka salad
lahsunwali double roti
mava ane badamnu pudding

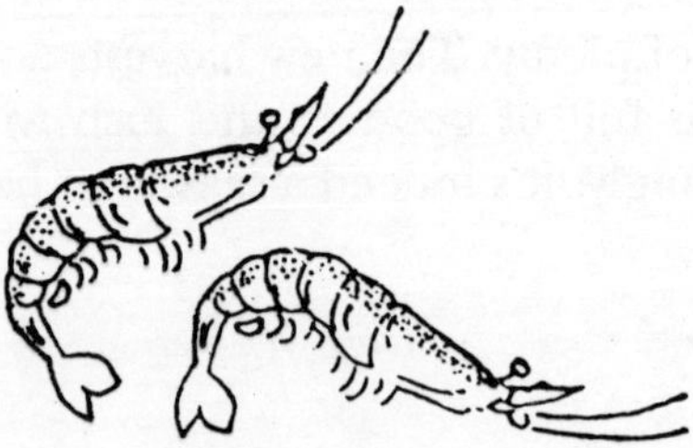

MURGH JARDALOOWALA

(Chicken Apricot Curry)

Serves: 6 **Cooking Time: 1 hr 30 mins**

- $1^1/_2$ kg. chicken, skinned, cut into serving pieces
- 2 onions, chopped
- 1 tbsp. garam masala powder
- 1 tsp. chilli powder
- 1 tsp. turmeric powder
- $^1/_2$ tsp. ginger-garlic paste
- 10 dried apricots, soaked in water, seeded, drained
- 1 cup coconut milk
- 1 tbsp. flour (*maida*)
- 1 tbsp. lemon juice
- 1 tbsp. brown sugar or caramel sauce
- 3 tbsp. cream
- $^3/_4$ litre chicken stock, made by boiling skins and bones (if any)

Heat 3 tbsp. oil. Stir fry chicken till brown. Reserve. Add remaining oil. Add onion and ginger-garlic paste. Brown. Add powdered spices and stock mixed well with flour. (Add the stock carefully to avoid lumps.) Add chicken and salt, lemon juice and sugar. Cook on a low flame till chicken is tender. Add coconut milk and apricots. Before serving, stir in cream.

JHINGA RAIWALA

(Prawns in Mustard Sauce)

Serves: 6 **Cooking Time: 1 hr**

1 kg. large prawns, shelled, cleaned
2 onions, ground
1/2 tsp. ginger-garlic paste
1/2 tsp. mustard paste
1/4 tsp. chilli powder
2 green chillies, ground
1/4 tsp. turmeric powder
1 tsp. mustard oil
1 tbsp. coriander leaves, chopped
Oil for cooking
Salt to taste

Mix onions, ginger-garlic, mustard and green chillies pastes. Mix the prawns with the paste, salt, chilli and turmeric powder and mustard oil. Place this mixture in the centre of the foil. Roast in medium oven for 45 minutes. Serve hot garnished with coriander leaves.

DALKA OSAMAN

(Dal Curry)

Serves: 6

Cooking Time: 45 mins

$^1/_2$ cup *toor* dal, (red gram dal) boiled soft with 2 cups stock
2 green chillies, chopped
1 tsp. turmeric powder
$^1/_2$ tsp. cumin seeds
$^1/_2$ tsp. mustard seeds
8 curry leaves
1 radish, sliced
3 cocum
1 tbsp. jaggery
1 tbsp. coriander leaves, chopped
3 tbsp. grated coconut
2 tsp. oil
Salt to taste

Boil dal stock with liquidised dal and add 2 cups water. Add green chillies, cocum, curry leaves, jaggery, salt, powdered spices, and cooked radish. Heat oil. Add mustard seeds and cumin seeds. When they pop, pour oil over dal. Add coconut and coriander leaves. Serve hot.

GARAM MASALE KA PIZZA

(Pizza with Indian Spices)

Serves: 6 **Cooking Time: 1 hr 30 mins**

3 tomatoes, chopped
2 capsicums, chopped
2 spring onions, chopped
1 tsp. ginger-garlic paste
1 small tin baked beans
1 tsp. garam masala powder
$^1/_2$ tsp. chilli powder
1 tsp. coriander leaves, chopped
Oil as needed
Salt to taste
8 pzza bases,readymade
2 cups cooking cheese,grated
$^1/_4$ cup chilli garlic sauce

Heat 3 tbsp. oil. Add onions. Stir fry. Add capsicums and tomatoes and stir fry till tender. Add powdered masalas and baked beans. Add salt and coriander leaves. Cover 8 pizza bases with the mixture. Cover each with the cheese and dot with sauce. Grill for 8 to 10 minutes and serve hot.

• •

CHAWAL KAJUDAR

(Cashew Rice)

Serves: 6 **Cooking Time: 1 hr**

2 cups *basmati* rice,
washed, drained
1 tsp. sugar
5 tbsp. broken cashewnuts
3 tbsp. oil
Salt to taste

Heat oil. Brown cashews. Remove and reserve. In the same oil add rice. Stir and add sugar and salt. Add $^3/_4$ of the cashews and 4 cups hot water. Cover and cook till rice is done. Garnish with remaining cashews.

FALONKA SALAD

(Waldorf Salad in Thousand Island Dressing)

Serves: 6 **Cooking Time: 1 hr**

1 cup pineapple slices
1 cup grapes
1 cup orange segments
1 cup apple chopped
1 cup walnuts, coarsely broken
1 cup boiled peas
1 cup boiled potatoes, peeled, chopped
2 cups mayonnaise
1 cup tomato ketchup
Salt to taste

Mix all ingredients and chill before serving.

• •

LAHSUNWALI DOUBLE ROTI

(Garlic Bread)

Serves: 6 **Cooking Time: 30 mins**

8 crisp bread rolls
$^1/_2$ cup butter
2 tsp. garlic paste

Mix butter and garlic. Slit rolls and fill with mixture. Heat through in a hot oven before serving.

MAVA ANE BADAMNU PUDDING

(Burnt Milk Almond Pudding)

Serves: 6 **Cooking Time: 1 hr 30 mins**

For the pastry shell:
4 egg yolks, separated
$^{1}/_{2}$ cup butter
$1^{1}/_{2}$ cup flour (*maida*)
2 tbsp. ground sugar
Iced water

For filling
$^{1}/_{2}$ cup butter
4 egg whites, separated
$1^{1}/_{4}$ kg. sweet *mava*
Almond and vanilla essence
1 tbsp. *charoli* seeds

Pastry

Mix butter and sugar with the palm of your hand till creamy. Add flour and roll into a breadcrumb-like mixture. Then add iced water—enough to make a stiff dough. Freeze for 30 minutes. Roll out and line a 30 cm. pie dish. Flute the edges. Prick the pastry base with a fork and bake in a moderately hot oven till firm. Remove. Reserve.

Filling

Beat butter and yolks together. Add softened ground *mava*, essence and ground almonds or cashews. Check sugar. Add stiffly beaten egg whites. Put into the shell, sprinkle *charoli* over and bake for 20 minutes or till golden and done. Check if a toothpick inserted comes out clean. Remove. Cool. Cut into slices and serve.

seasonal entertainment

HEMANT RITU

(Autumn Luxury)

Burnished gold, gentle muted copper and green turning slowly yellow—these are the colours of the most mellow and nostalgic season of the year—autumn. The sun-dried crisp leaves tumble down from trees in cascades and make a crackling carpet in the gardens. Early morning dew falls on coppery leaves to lend them a crystalline sheen and a magical touch of moisture.

This is the season of outdoor eating, of entertaining your guests to music and a repast which makes the most of the seasonal produce of fruits and vegetables. Early in autumn, white and fresh cauliflowers, tender green peas and plump and juicy tomatoes begin to flood the market and it's time to enjoy the bounty of nature to the fullest. Stuffed vegetables, sweets and *halwas* made from fruits and vegetables present a pleasing array for the palate in this season. The table decoration can also reflect this copper-gold grandeur by use of leaf or fruit motifs in linen and crockery. In early autumn picnics in forest glades and lakeside resorts, spell an enchanted spell of entertaining.

menu

masale ka moussaka
gol aloo dum ke
taktaki roti
moong ki dahibadi
yakhni pulao
naspati badam ka mitha

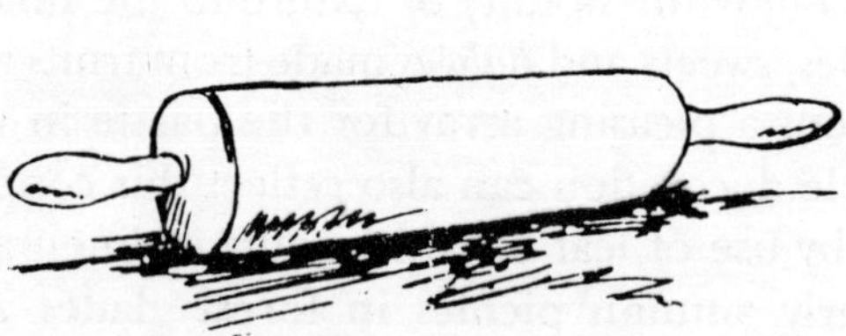

MASALE KA MOUSSAKA

(Moussaka Indian Style)

Serves: 6 **Cooking Time: 1 hr 30 mins**

1 big brinjal, sliced
2 potatoes, peeled, sliced
4 cups crushed toast or breadcrumbs
$^1/_2$ cup cheese, grated
Oil as needed
Salt and pepper to taste

For filling
$^3/_4$ kg. minced meat
2 onions grated
1 tsp. ginger-garlic paste
1 tsp. chilli powder
$^1/_2$ tsp. turmeric powder
1 tsp. garam masala powder
1 cup coriander leaves, chopped
1 cup tomato *puree*
Oil as needed
Salt to taste

For toppings
$^3/_4$ cup flour (maida)
2 cups milk
$^1/_2$ cup cream
$^1/_2$ tsp. nutmeg, ground
$^1/_2$ cup grated cheese
2 eggs, beaten
Salt and pepper to taste

Marinate brinjal and potato slices in salt and fry in hot oil till soft. Drain and reserve. To the oil in the pan, add some more if needed to make $^1/_2$ cup.

When hot add grated onion and ginger-garlic paste. Brown.Add mince and stir fry till brown. Add tomato *puree*, all powder spices, salt, pepper and coriander leaves (leaving some for decoration) and pressure cook till done. Open. Stir till dry. Reserve.

Heat 2 tbsp. oil. Add flour and cook just till raw smell disappears. Add milk and heat till no lumps remain. Add cream, nutmeg and salt. When creamy, remove. Cool a while and add cheese and egg. Blend well.

Now in a baking dish, put a layer of brinjal and potato slices. Add PA some breadcrumbs and cheese. Put a layer of mince over this. Continue the layers till vegetables and meat are over, the top layer being of brinjals. Pour the cheese sauce evenly over the *moussaka* and bake till the layers are set and the top is golden. Remove and serve garnished with coriander leaves.

GOL ALOO DUM KE

(Whole Potatoes in Yoghurt Sauce)

Serves: 6 **Cooking Time: 1 hr**

1 kg. small potatoes, boiled, peeled
1 tsp. cumin seeds
1 tsp. coriander powder
1 tsp. chilli powder
$^1/_2$ tsp. turmeric powder
1 tsp. garam masala
1 pinch asafoetida
$^1/_2$ tsp. grated ginger
1 cup yoghurt
1 tbsp.coriander leaves, chopped
A small ball of dough
$^1/_2$ cup oil
Salt to taste

Heat the oil. Add ginger and asafoetida. Prick the potatoes all round and fry in oil till brown. Drain and reserve. From the remaining oil, heat 2 tbsp. Add cumin seeds. Add yoghurt and all powder masalas. Add salt and stir till gravy is thick. Add drained potatoes, $^1/_2$ cup water and cover. Seal the lid over the pot with dough . Cook over low heat till potatoes are spongy and the gravy is light. Serve garnished with coriander leaves.

TAKTAKI ROTI

(Gramflour Roti)

Serves: 6 **Cooking Time: 1 hr**

2 cups gram flour (*besan*)
1 cup whole wheat flour (*atta*)
$^1/_2$ tsp. cumin seeds, coarsely ground
1 tbsp. coriander leaves, chopped
1 tsp. small pieces of green chilli skins
2 tbsp. oil
Ghee
Salt to taste

Mix all ingredients with 2 tbsp. oil and enough water to make a stiff dough. Make into lemon-sized balls. Roll out each on a floured board and cook on a greased griddle till crisp and golden. Serve with ghee.

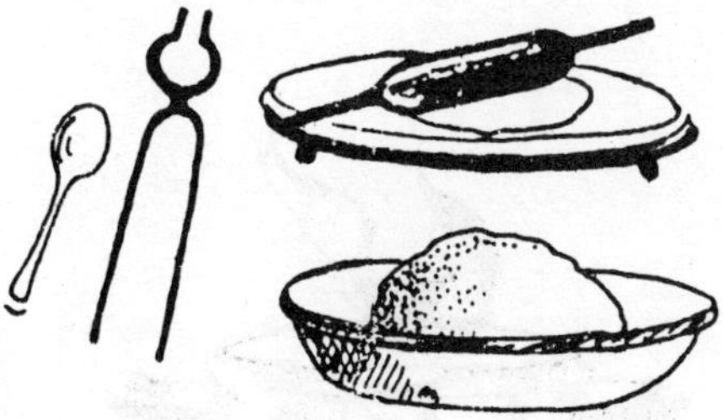

MOONG KI DAHIBADI

(Lentil Dumplings in Yoghurt)

Serves: 6 **Cooking Time: 1 hr**

250 gm. *moong* dal with skins, water for soaked in 4 hours, drained, ground
4 cups yoghurt
$^1/_4$ tsp. asafoetida
1 tsp. cumin seeds, roasted, ground
1 tbsp.coriander leaves, chopped
1 green chilli, minced
2 tbsp. sweet chutney
Oil
Salt and sugar to taste

Add salt to batter of dal. Add asafoetida and beat till frothy. Heat oil and fry small drops of batter till crisp and done. Drain and put in water. Beat yoghurt well. Add salt and sugar. Add moong *badis* after squeezing out all water, keeping them whole. Add chilli, coriander, sprinkle cumin powder and sweet chutney on top.

(Make sweet chutney by mixing $^1/_2$ cup tamarind pulp and $^1/_2$ cup jaggery and boiling mixture till smooth. Cool.)

YAKHNI PULAO

(Stock Cooked Rice)

Serves: 6 **Cooking Time: 1 hr**

$^1/_2$ kg. mutton, cubed, boneless
2 long pieces cinnamon
4 cardamoms
2 bay leaves
4 cloves
2 cup *basmati* rice, washed, drained
1 tsp. chilli powder
$^1/_2$ tsp. cumin seeds
2 tbsp. ghee
Salt to taste

Boil meat with whole spices and salt in $1^1/_2$ litres of water. Pressure cook if necessary. Remove meat and reserve.

Heat two tbsp. ghee. Add meat and brown. Add rice and brown. Add cumin seeds, chilli powder and salt if needed. Add the meat stock and water to make the level 2 cm. above the level of rice. Fix lid tightly and cook slowly till rice is done and fluffy.

NASPATI BADAM KA MITHA

(Pear and Almond Bake)

Serves 6: **Cooking Time: 1 hr 30 mins**

$^3/_4$ cup butter
$^3/_4$ cup ground sugar
3 eggs
5 tbsp. powdered almonds
$1^1/_4$ cup flour (*maida*)
$^1/_4$ cup milk
2 pears, peeled, sliced
2 tbsp. almonds, thinly sliced

For custard
2 tbsp. plain custard powder
4 tbsp. sugar
2 tsp. ginger powder
2 tbsp. butter

Beat butter and sugar together till frothy. Add eggs, one at a time. Add almond powder, flour and milk gradually to make a thick batter.

Make custard by mixing powder with sugar and ginger. Add milk and mix well so that there are no lumps. Stir over heat till smooth and creamy. Add the butter. In a baking dish, pour the cooled custard. Arrange pears over. Pour cake batter on top and sprinkle sliced almonds. Bake in a medium oven till golden and moist. Serve with extra custard if liked. (In that case, double the custard quantity.)

seasonal entertainment

SHISHIR RITU

(Winter Opulence)

In every region of India, winter spells good eating. Outdoor life comes almost to a standstill. In the freezing winters of the north, the fields of mustard greens are ready for harvesting. So are pearly rich corncobs. So *rotis* made from golden corn flour and a butter-bathed green *saag* made from mustard leaves is the speciality of this season.

In the west, a large number of root vegetables, enhanced in taste by green garlic and fresh ginger, are used for creating outstanding dishes like *Oondhiyoon*. Ponk, which is tender grain eaten with a chilli-spiked chutney and sugar granules, is also a winter speciality.

In the coastal regions of the peninsula, *hurda* or tender corn is gently roasted in coal and wood fires and is eaten in *barbecue*-like farmhouse parties. Sugarcane juice, new malt jaggery and tender coconut cooked in treacle syrup are farm delicacies which travellers stop by to eat.

Winter is indeed a good season for gourmet cooking and gorgeous entertaining!

menu

Bhuna Shahed ka Murgh
chutneywali machchi
aloo matar malai curry
baide ke chawal
sem ka beansproutwala salad
paratha kali mirch

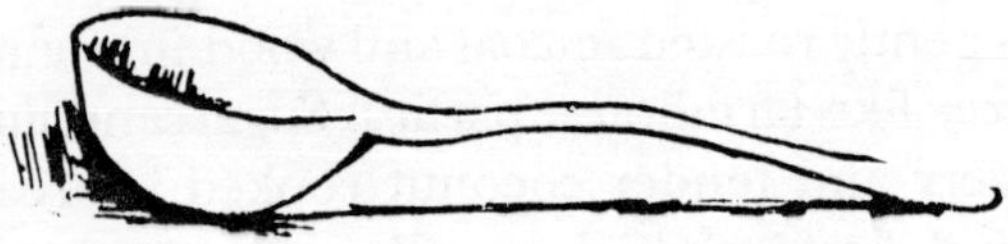

BHUNA SHAHED KA MURGH

(Honey Barbecued Chicken)

Serves: 6 **Cooking Time: 1 hr 30 mins**

6 legs of chicken, skinned, cleaned
2 tsp. tandoor masala
1 tsp. chilli powder
1 tsp. turmeric powder
1 tsp. *kasoori methi*
1 tbsp. honey
1 tsp. ginger-garlic paste
1 tbsp. tomato ketchup
4 tbsp. oil
Foil
Salt to taste

Mix all ingredients and marinate chicken in the mixture. Line a baking tray with foil and arrange chicken pieces. Pour juices over and cover with foil. Bake in a medium oven till done. Then grill, after removing top foil till the top is crisp. Serve with *parathas.*

CHUTNEYWALI MACHCHI

(Fish with Chutney)

Serves: 6 **Cooking Time: 45 mins**

3 large pomfrets, cleaned
slit across
1 cup chutney

$^1/_4$ cup oil
Banana leaves
Salt to taste

To make chutney:
2 cups coriander leaves,
1 cup mint (*pudina*) leaves
1 tsp. sugar

A small ball tamarind or 1 tsp. lemon juice
2 tbsp. grated coconut
Salt to taste

Grind all the chutney ingredients together till smooth. Keep aside. Rub salt over the fish on the inside and outside and leave for half an hour. Then stuff with the chutney and wrap in banana leaves. Gently steam till done or cook in an oven till soft. Serve with rice.

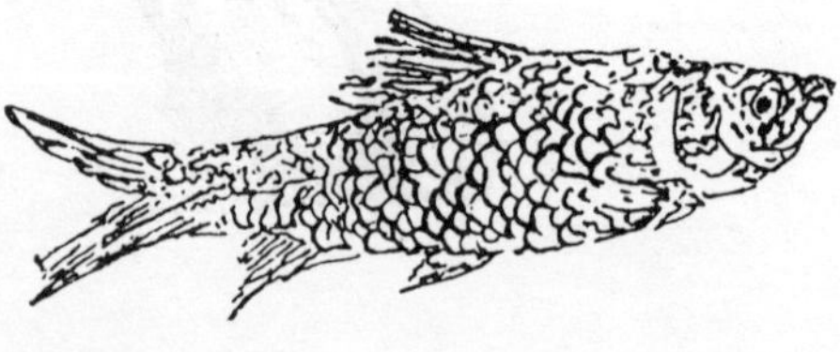

ALOO MATAR MALAI CURRY

(Peas Potato Cream Curry)

Serves: 6 **Cooking Time: 1 hr**

3 large potatoes, peeled, cubed
1 cup peas, cooked slightly
1/2 cup cream
1/2 cup ground onions
1 tsp. ginger-garlic paste
1/2 cup ketchup or tomato *puree*
15 cashewnuts, soaked in water
1 tsp. garam masala
1 tsp. chilli powder
1 tsp. *amchur* (mango)powder
1/2 cup oil
1/2 cup coriander leaves
Salt and sugar to taste

Heat oil. Add cashews and potatoes. Stir fry till brown. Add onion and ginger-garlic paste. Stir till oil separates. Add peas. Cook till vegetables are done. Add tomato *puree* and all powder masalas. Stir till done. Add salt, sugar and coriander leaves. Serve with rice after sprinkling cream.

• •

BAIDE KE CHAWAL

(Egg Pulao)

Serves: 6 **Cooking Time: 1 hr**

6 eggs, boiled, shelled
2 cups basmati rice, washed
1 stick cinnamon
5 cloves
5 cardamoms
1 tsp. cumin seeds
5 tbsp. oil
Salt to taste

Heat 1 tbsp. oil. Stir fry whole eggs till golden. Reserve. Add rest of oil. Fry spices and cumin seeds. Add rice and stir till translucent. Add 4 cups hot water and salt. Cover and cook till rice is done. When done, arrange in a dish with eggs on top and serve hot.

SEM KA BEANSPROUTWALA SALAD

(Beans and Beansprouts)

Serves: 6

Cooking Time: 1 hr

$^1/_2$ kg. french beans, threads removed, sliced finely, diagonally, steamed
1 cup sprouted *moong* beans, steamed
1 tsp. cumin seeds
1 tbsp. peanuts, roasted, crushed
$^1/_2$ tsp. turmeric powder
1 tsp. lemon juice
1 tsp. oil
1 tsp. sugar
Salt to taste

Heat oil. Add cumin seeds. Add beans and sprouts. Add turmeric powder, salt and sugar. Add peanuts. Stir till blended. Add lemon juice and serve with rice.

• •

PARATHA KALI MIRCH

(Black pepper parathao)

Serves: 6

Cooking Time: 1 hr

3 cups wholewheat flour (*atta*)
$^1/_2$ cup oil
$^1/_4$ tsp. turmeric powder
10 peppercorns, crushed
Salt to taste

Knead a dough of all ingredients adding water when needed. Make into lemon-sized balls. Roll out into 12 cm. *parathas* and fry on a griddle on both sides till done. Serve with chicken.

business entertainment

Giving lunches, dinners or cocktail parties for the enhancement of one's business interests has become an accepted fact in today's success-oriented society. Very often, an upmarket executive—man or woman—entertains colleagues or customers to restaurants or hotels for this purpose. On many occasions, however, home entertaining is compulsory and perhaps even more useful. Modern young couples, who had little time during their academic life or early career years to learn the art of being hosts, have therefore to pay special attention to this aspect. How do they make their homes more warm, welcoming and hospitable ? By paying attention to detail. The food, the ambience and the *camraderie* in a home makes hospitality an exciting adventure and no family should miss the glow of success such entertaining generates. Here are a few ideas on how to plan business buffets or dinners.

menu–I

hari pattika murgh
gosht rashida
moong dal ki tikiya
dalonka pulao
rum ka pudding

menu–II

jhinga pulao
aloo ka chow chow
phoolgobhi ka bharta
dhania ke parathe
moongphali ka chatpata
alu matar ka pie
bhutte ke kabab
malai ka aam

menu–III

gosht kolhapuri
simla mirch baingan rizla
pattionki dal
hare narangi kabab
matar ke chawal
dashami chhoti roti
aam ki lanji chutney
jelly ka jhag

menu–IV

murgh ka mirchwala stroganoff
goa ki khatti machchi curry
doodh ke chawal
sabzika mitha stew
bhuni saabziyan
ananas ka malai salad
seb ke pancake aur icecream

HARI PATTIKA MURGH

(Chicken Leek Curry)

Serves: 6 **Cooking Time: 1 hr 30 mins**

6 large chicken legs, skinned
$^1/_2$ cup flour (maida)
1 tsp. chilli powder
1 tsp. mustard powder
2 tsp. pepper
Oil for frying
Salt to taste

For sauce:
8 tomatoes
1 tbsp. garlic paste
2 cups spring onions, chopped
12 mushrooms, chopped
12 walnut kernels, crushed
Oil and salt as needed

Cook tomatoes and pass through a sieve to get juice. Heat 5 tbsp. oil. Add mushrooms. Fry and reserve. Fry walnuts. Drain and reserve. Add garlic and onions. Add tomato juice and mushrooms and walnuts. Season with salt and simmer till blended.

Now roll chicken pieces in a mixture of flour, chilli, mustard and pepper powder. Fry in hot oil and remove. Pressure cook in a little water for 7 minutes till done. Add chicken and gravy to tomato mixture. Blend well and serve.

GOSHT RASHIDA

(Mutton in Gravy)

Serves: 6 **Cooking Time: 1 hr 30 mins**

600 gm. boneless mutton, cubed
3 onions, grated
1 tbsp. ginger-garlic paste
1 tbsp. coriander/cumin powder
1 tbsp. chilli powder
1 tsp. turmeric powder
1 tbsp. garam masala
$^1/_2$ cup yoghurt
2 tomatoes, chopped
1 tsp. peppercorns, cloves, cinnamon
$^1/_2$ cup oil
$^1/_2$ cup coriander leaves, chopped
Salt to taste

Steam meat till tender. Reserve. Heat oil. Fry onion and whole spices till brown. Add tomato. Then add yoghurt, powder spices and fry till oil separates. Add salt and meat. Blend till gravy is thick. Garnish with coriander leaves and serve with rice.

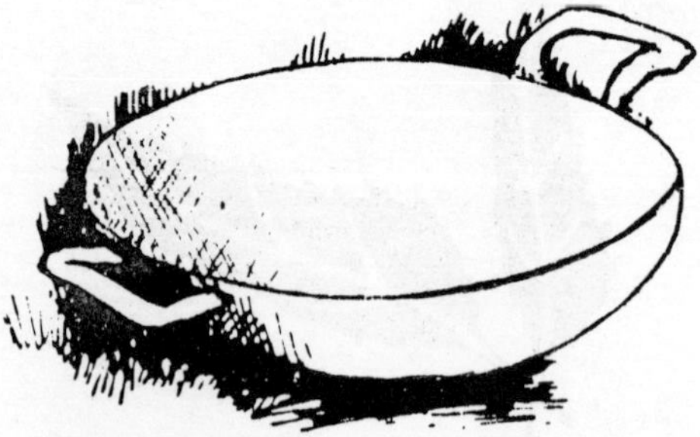

MOONG DAL KI TIKIYA

(Dal Cutlets)

Serves: 6 **Cooking Time: 1 hr**

500 gm. *moong* dal,soaked in water, drained
1 tbsp. garam masala powder
4 eggs
1 tsp. green chilli paste
1 cup breadcrumbs
$^1/_2$ cup gram flour (*besan*)
2 onions, grated
2 tsp. yoghurt
Oil
Salt to taste

Grind dal to a paste. Heat 2 tbsp. oil. Fry onions. Add to paste. Roast gram flour and garam masala dry and add to paste. Add chilli paste, yoghurt, beaten eggs, salt and knead. Make flat cutlets and fry after rolling in breadcrumbs, in hot oil. Serve with rice and curry.

DALONKA PULAO

(Lentil Rice)

Serves: 6 **Cooking Time: 1 hr**

1 cup mixed whole dals, i.e, *moong, masoor, chana,* soaked in water, drained
$1^1/_2$ cups *basmati* rice
2 tsp. coriander-cumin powder
2 tbsp. *copra,* grated
1 tsp. turmeric powder
1 tsp. garam masala
1 tsp. chilli powder
3 cloves garlic
2 tomatoes, chopped
$^1/_2$ cup mint leaves
Oil
Salt to taste

Steam cook all dals separately in salt water till just done. Heat 4 tbsp. oil. Add onion and fry. Add all powder spices and garlic and coconut. Toss. Add rice and salt. Add tomatoes. Stir and add 5 cups hot water. Cook till fluffy and donc. Add dals and mix well. Heat through and serve with yoghurt.

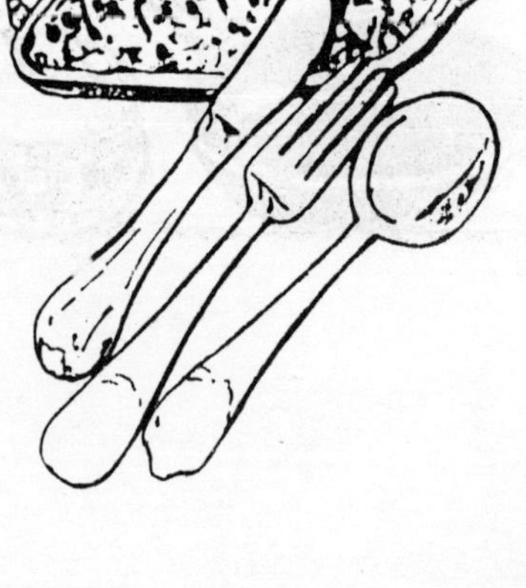

Summer lunch by the window

Table laid in ethnic style

The Janamashtami variety menu

Holi : Colours and Sweets

Chicken Rice : Varieties of Rice are a staple of Indian entertaining.

Mango days are happy days in India.
May-June are the months of mango drinks, puddings, sherbets, ice-creams.

RUM KA PUDDING

(Club Souffle)

Serves: 6 **Cooking Time: 1 hr 30 mins**

$3^1/_2$ cups milk
6 eggs
6 tbsp. sugar
5 tbsp. gelatin
1 tbsp. wine or rum
1 cup cream
1 small chocolate

Heat milk. When slightly cool, add beaten egg yolks and sugar and make custard. Melt gelatine in warm water and add to custard. Freeze for $^1/_2$ hour. Remove and add stiffly beaten egg whites, cream and rum. Blend and freeze. When ready, unmould, cover with grated chocolate and serve chilled.

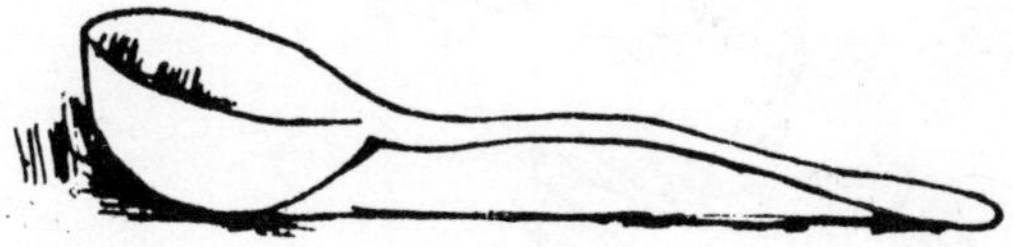

JHINGA PULAO

(Prawn Rice)

Serves: 6 **Cooking Time 1 hr 30 mins**

- $1^1/_2$ cup *basmati* rice, washed drained
- 2 cups prawns, deveined, cleaned
- $^1/_2$ tsp. ginger paste
- 3 tbsp. oil
- 2 cloves garlic, chopped
- 4 onions, chopped
- 2 tsp. chilli powder
- 2 tsp. chilli vinegar or Worcester sauce
- 2 tomatoes, blanched, juice removed
- 1 carrot, peeled, cut into strips
- Salt to taste

Cook rice in salt water till done. Drain out water. Cook carrot till just done. Heat oil and fry onioins, garlic and ginger. Add prawns, chilli powder and salt. Cook till done. Add tomato juice. Stir till blended.

Mix rice with prawns, carrots, sauce and salt if needed. Blend well and heat through before serving.

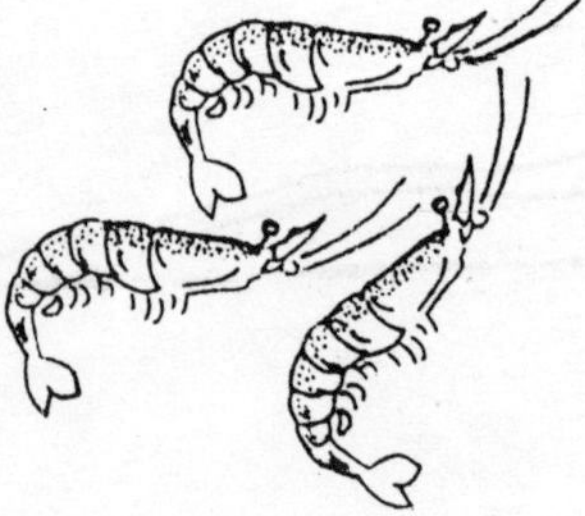

ALOO KA CHOW CHOW

(Potato Chow Chow)

Serves: 6 **Cooking Time: 45 mins**

$^1/_2$ kg. small potatoes, boiled, peeled
$^1/_4$ kg. french beans, strings removed, halved
2 carrots, peeled, cut into strips
1 tbsp. mustard seeds
$^1/_2$ tsp. fenugreek seeds
$^1/_4$ tsp. asafoetida
10 red chillies
$^1/_2$ tsp. turmeric powder
1 tbsp. lemon juice
$^1/_4$ cup oil
Salt to taste

Heat $^1/_2$ tsp. oil. Fry mustard and fenugreek seeds and red chillies. Add turmeric and asafoetida and grind to a fine paste. Heat remaining oil. Add carrots and beans. Fry till soft. Add salt, ground paste and cook till crisp but done. Add whole potatoes and lemon juice. This may be served cold or hot.

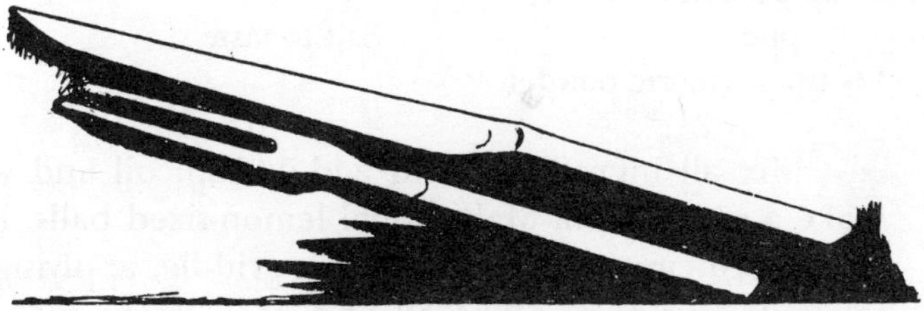

PHOOLGOBHI KA BHARTA

(Cauliflower Yoghurt)

Serves: 6 **Cooking Time: 30 mins**

- $^1/_2$ kg. cauliflower cleaned, flowerettes chopped, boiled in salt water
- 4 cups yoghurt, beaten
- 2 green chillies, minced
- 1 cup bread crouton (fried bread pieces)
- 1 cup coriander leaves, chopped
- $^1/_2$ cup raisins, soaked in water, drained
- 1 tsp. sugar
- Salt to taste

Mix all ingredients in the yoghurt and chill. Just before serving, add croutons and sprinkle with coriander leaves.

• •

DHANIA KE PARATHE

(Coriander Leaf Roti)

Serves: 6 **Cooking Time: 1 hr**

- 3 cups whole wheat flour
- 1 cup coriander leaves, chopped
- $^1/_2$ tsp. turmeric powder
- $^1/_2$ tsp. cumin seeds
- Oil
- Salt to taste

Mix all ingredients and add 1 tbsp. oil and water to make a stiff dough. Make equal lemon-sized balls. Roll out each to 10 cm. circles and fry on a griddle, applying a little oil to the griddle. Make all and keep warm till ready to serve.

MOONGPHALI KA CHATPATA

(Peanut Chutney)

Serves: 6 **Cooking Time: 15 mins**

2 cups roasted salted peanuts
12 garlic cloves, minced
1 tsp. chilli powder
$^{1}/_{2}$ tsp. tamarind paste
1 tsp. sugar
Salt to taste

Put all ingredients into a mixie and grind to a coarse mixture—a powder. Bottle when cool and serve as an accompaniment.

• •

ALU MATAR KA PIE

(Pea Pie)

Serves: 6 **Cooking Time: 1 hr 30 mins**

8 potatoes, boiled, peeled
1 cup peas, cooked
3 tbsp. oil
$^{1}/_{4}$ cup breadcrumbs
1 tsp. ginger, shredded
2 green chillies, minced
1 cup cheese, shredded
3 eggs, beaten
1 cup coriander leaves, chopped
Salt and pepper to taste

Rub oil on the inside of a pie dish and cover with crumbs. Knead potatoes into a dough with a little oil and salt. Add $^{1}/_{2}$ of ginger, chillies, cheese, coriander leaves and pepper. Divide into 2 balls. Roll out one ball and cover the bottom of the pie dish. Mix peas with remaining ingredients leaving a little cheese and mix with beaten egg. Put into the potato case. Cover with remaining potato mixture. Brush with egg and top with cheese. Bake in a medium oven till done. Slice and serve warm.

BHUTTE KE KABAB

(Corn Rolls)

Serves: 6 **Cooking Time: 1 hr 30 mins**

$1^1/_2$ cup corn kernels, cooked
3 green chillies, minced
1 cup coriander leaves, chopped
1 tsp. ginger paste
1 tsp. garam masala
$^1/_2$ cup chick pea flour (*besan*)
Oil
Salt to taste

Crush corn. Mix with chillies, coriander leaves, ginger and garam masala. Add salt and grind to bind. Add a little hot oil and blend with *besan.* Form into *kabab* shapes and deep fry in batches till golden. Serve hot with chutney.

MALAI KA AAM

(Cream Mango)

Serves: 6 **Cooking Time: 1 hr**

$^{1}/_{2}$ litre milk
4 tbsp. sugar
$4^{1}/_{2}$ tsp. cornflour mixed with 4 tbsp. milk
16 Marie biscuits
3 mangoes,peeled, sliced
$^{3}/_{4}$ cup cream mixed with 2 tsp. castor sugar

Heat milk with sugar and slowly add smooth cornflour mixture. When mixture is thick, remove and cool. Crush biscuits and line a pudding bowl bottom with the powder. Mix a few chopped mango pieces and the dripping mango juice with milk mixture and pour over crumb layer. Freeze. Cover with whipped cream and decorate with remaining mango slices. Chill before serving.

GOSHT KOLHAPURI

(Mutton Curry)

Serves: 6 **Cooking Time: 1 hr**

1 kg. mutton, cubed
$^1/_4$ fresh coconut, grated
$^1/_4$ dry copra, grated
2 tsp. garam masala
2 tsp. chilli powder
1 tsp. turmeric powder
3 large onions, sliced
3 tomatoes, chopped
8 peppercorns
8 cloves
8 cardamoms
1 tbsp.coriander seeds
1 tbsp. ginger-garlic paste
4 potatoes, peeled,halved
$^1/_2$ cup oil
Salt to taste

Heat a little oil. Add cloves, cardamoms, coriander seeds, peppercorns. Add onions, garlic and ginger. Brown. Add both grated coconut and tomato. Roast to brown. Cool. Grind to a fine paste. Heat remaining oil. Add meat with powder spices and salt and stir fry till brown. Add spice paste and 2 cups of water. Add potatoes and pressure cook for 15 minutes till done. Serve with *roti.*

SIMLA MIRCH BAINGAN RIZLA

(Brinjal Capsicum Curry)

Serves: 6 **Cooking Time: 1 hr**

8 small brinjals, sliced
6 small capsicums, sliced
1 tsp. turmeric powder
1 tsp. chilli powder
1 tsp. garam masala powder
1 tsp. cumin seeds
1 cup tomato *puree*
1 cup coriander leaves
8 curry leaves
Oil for frying
Salt to taste

Ground to a paste:
$^1/_2$ cup roasted peanuts
1 pod garlic
1 large onions
2.5 cm. piece ginger
1 tbsp. sesame seeds
$^1/_2$ cup coconut,grated

Deep fry brinjal and capsicum. Drain on paper. In 4 tbsp.of oil, add turmeric, chilli and garam masala powders. Add vegetables and stir fry till soft. Add tomato and ground paste and salt. Blend. Heat 2 tbsp. oil. Add cumin seeds and curry leaves. Pour over *Rizla.* Garnish with coriander leaves and serve.

PATTIONKI DAL

(Leafy Dal)

Serves: 6 **Cooking Time: 1 hr**

1 cup tuvar dal, soaked in water
2 cup fenugreek leaves, minced
1 cup spinach leaves, minced
1 cup coriander leaves, minced
6 garlic cloves
1 tsp. turmeric powder
1 tomato, minced
3 green chillies, minced
3 tsp. oil
Salt to taste

Cook dal with all leaves, tomato, green chillies, turmeric and salt till soft. Churn and blend. Heat oil. Add minced garlic. Brown and pour over dal. Serve with rice.

HARE NARANGI KABAB

(Green/Orange Coloured Kababs)

Serves: 6 **Cooking Time: 1 hr**

$1^1/_2$ cups *chana* dal, soaked in water, drained
3 green chillies, minced
$^1/_2$ tsp. turmeric powder
$^1/_2$ tsp. garam masala powder
1 cup coriander leaves, minced
$^1/_2$ cup coconut, ground
$^1/_2$ cup spinach, cooked, ground
$^1/_4$ tsp. soda bi carb
Oil
Salt and pepper to taste

Grind half the dal coarsely. The other half finely. Add a pinch of soda bi carb to each portion.

To the coarse paste add half of chillies, turmeric, half of coriander leaves, coconut, salt and pepper. Make flat balls and deep fry in hot oil. In the fine paste, add garam masala, remaining chillies, coriander leaves, spinach, salt and pepper. Make flat balls and deep fry in hot oil. Arrange in alternate layers while serving.

• •

MATAR KE CHAWAL

(Pea Pulao)

Serves: 6 **Cooking Time: 45 mins**

$1^1/_2$ cups *basmati* rice, washed, drained
1 tsp. cumin seeds
1 cup peas
2 tbsp. oil
Salt to taste

Heat oil. Add cumin seeds. Add rice and peas and salt. Stir fry. Add 4 cups hot water and cook covered till done.

DASHAMI CHHOTI ROTI

(Mini Yoghurt Rotis)

Serves: 6 **Cooking Time: 1 hr**

3 cups whole wheat flour (*atta*)
1 tsp. cumin seeds
$^1/_2$ tsp. turmeric powder
$^1/_2$ cup yoghurt
$^1/_4$ tsp. asafoetida
1 tbsp. oil
Salt to taste

Knead all ingredients together in a stiff dough adding water if needed. Make small balls and roll out *puri*-sized *rotis*. Cook on a greased griddle one by one and serve with butter.

• •

AAM KI LANJI CHUTNEY

(Sweet Mango Pickle)

Serves: 6 **Cooking Time: 1 hr**

3 large raw mangoes, peeled, chopped
$^1/_2$ cup raisins
1 cup vinegar
2 cups sugar
1 tbsp.roasted cumin seeds
1 tbsp. chilli powder
1 tsp. onion seeds (*kalonji*)

Heat vinegar and sugar. Add mangoes and raisins. Cook and add all spices. Cook till thick and shiny. Cool and serve.

JELLY KA JHAG

(Jelly Fruit Frost)

Serves: 6 **Cooking Time: 1 hr**

1 packet strawberry jelly
1 cup cream
5 glace cherries
2 cups mixed fruit, chopped
(pineapple, pears, grapes etc)

Make jelly as per instructions but with $^1/_2$ the water. Cool. Hold the pot over ice cubes and whisk vigorously till frothy. Continue till cold. Add cream and fold in without churning so cream does not curdle. Arrange fruit in a bowl. Pour frost over and set in the fridge. Decorate with cherry slices before serving chilled.

MURGH KA MIRCHWALA STROGANOFF

(Spicy Chicken Stroganoff)

Serves: 6 **Cooking Time: 1 hr 30 mins**

1 kg. chicken, boneless cubes cooked
2 tbsp. flour (*maida*)
1 tsp. chilli powder
1 cup cream
1 cup shredded cheese
2 tbsp. sugar
8 mushrooms
2 green chillies, minced
$^1/_4$ cup butter
Salt and pepper to taste

Heat butter. Add flour and stir till slightly golden. Add 2 cups water. Churn to avoid lumps. Add salt and pepper and ketchup. When sauce is creamy, add sugar and stir-fried mushrooms. Add chicken pieces and chilli powder. Remove and cool for 30 minutes. Stir in cream. Pour into a baking dish and cover with cheese. Cook in a hot oven till cheese melts. Serve hot.

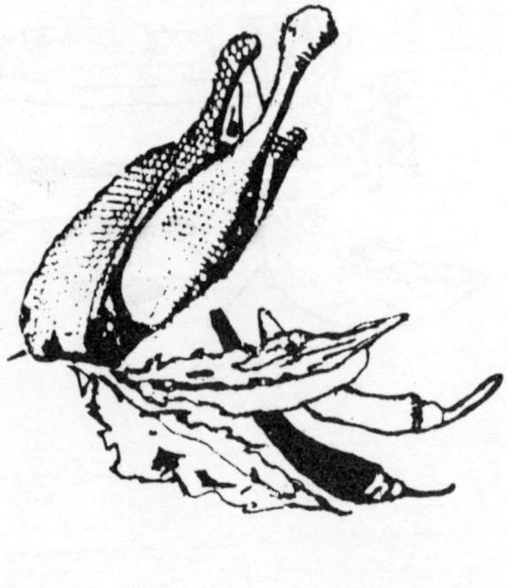

GOA KI KHATTI MACHCHI CURRY

(Goa Fish Curry)

Serves: 6 **Cooking Time: 1 hr**

2 pomfrets, cleaned, heads & tails removed, sliced
3 cups coconut, grated
1 tsp. turmeric powder
2 tsp. chilli powder
1 tsp. coriander seeds
3 *cocums* or peeled raw mango pieces (if in season)
2 tbsp. oil
Salt to taste

Wash fish slices and marinate in turmeric, chilli powder and salt to taste. Liquidise coconut and extract first thick milk ($1^1/_2$ cups) and then thin milk (1 cup).

Heat oil. Add fish and turn without breaking. Add thin coconut milk and *cocum* or mango. Cook till done. Add thick coconut milk. Boil once only and serve hot with rice.

DOODH KE CHAWAL

(Milk Rice)

Serves: 6 **Cooking Time: 1 hr**

- $1^1/_2$ cups *basmati* rice, soaked in water for 30 mins, drained
- $^1/_2$ cup milk

Add $2^1/_2$ cups water to milk and heat. Add rice and cook covered on a very low flame till rice is cooked. Stir occasionally and add water if needed. Cook till dry and fluffy. Serve with curry.

SABZI KA MITHA STEW

(Sweet Vegetable Stew)

Serves: 6

Cooking Time: 1 hr

3 tbsp. grated fresh coconut
3 cloves
3 stick cinnamon
2 tbsp. flour (*maida*)
1 cup peas, boiled
2 potatoes, boiled, peeled, cubed
2 tomatoes, choppped
1 cup coriander leaves, chopped
3 green chillies, dropped
2 onions, chopped
2 tsp. sugar
3 tbsp. oil
Salt to taste

Heat 1 tsp. oil. Gently fry cloves, cinnamon and coconut till golden. Remove. Reserve. Roast the flour in the same pan. Grind both with enough water to make a thick paste. Reserve. Heat remaining oil. Add onion and green chillies. Fry till golden. Add peas, potatoes, sugar, salt and tomatoes. Stir till tomatoes are soft. Add liquidized paste and enough water to make a thick gravy. Simmer and garnish with coriander leaves. Serve with bread.

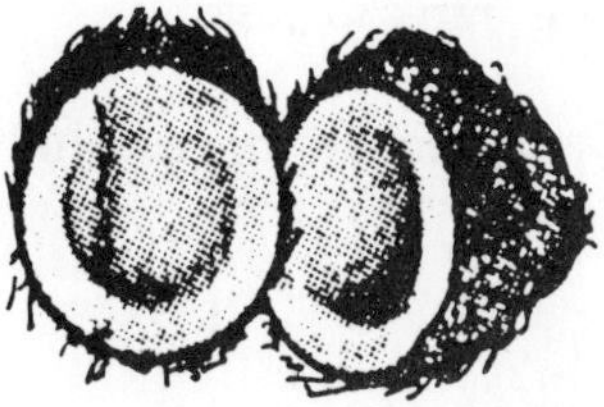

BHUNI SABZIYAN

(Fried Vegetables)

Serves: 6 **Cooking Time: 1 hr**

250 gm lady fingers, sliced thinly
2 brinjals, chopped into tiny cubes
3 potatoes, peeled, cut into fine cubes
2 tbsp. coarse powder of roasted peanuts
Oil
Salt, chilli powder and pepper to taste

Heat oil and fry one vegetable at a time. Drain and keep in a pan. Mix all three just before serving. Heat and add peanut powder, salt, chilli powder and pepper to taste.

• •

ANANAS KA MALAI SALAD

(Pineapple Cream Salad)

Serves: 6 **Cooking Time: 30 mins**

3 cups pineapple pieces
2 cups grated coconut, ground to paste
1 tsp. chilli powder
2 tsp. sugar or jaggery
Salt to taste

Mix all ingredients and chill completely before serving.

SEB KE PANCAKE AUR ICE CREAM

(Apple Pancakes with Ice-Cream)

erves: 6 **Cooking Time: 1 hr**

- cups flour (*maida*)
- apples, peeled, chopped
- tbsp. raisins, soaked in water, drained
- tsp. lemon juice
- /2 tsp. cinnamon powder
- /4 cup sugar
- 2 eggs, beaten
- Milk as needed
- Ghee
- A pinch of salt
- Vanila Ice-cream

Cook apples, raisins and sugar with lemon juice till soft nd pulpy. Add cinnamon and cook till dry. Reserve.

Mix flour, beaten eggs and enough milk to make a atter. Beat well and add a pinch of salt.

Grease a griddle. Pour one ladle of batter. Spread into thin round. Cover and cook. Open. Put a spoon of apple lling in the centre and roll over from both ends. Remove o a platter. Cook all pancakes like this and serve cold with cecream.

ethnic theme parties

There is no doubt that India's stupendously varied cuisine is almost a wonder of the world. Travel only a few miles away from your town and the flavours change, the taste changes and even the colour and shape of food changes so elusively that one is left wondering at the sheer variety of ingredients, spices, methods of cooking and the art of serving. Not only does each region have its own cuisine, each community also has its own way of using local vegetables or spices to create specialities which rate high in taste, flavour and aesthetic appeal.

Many are the communities who have migrated to India during the past centuries for various cultural and political reasons, mingled with this vast river of humanity, still maintaining their identity and individuality in food habits. For example, though Parsis have lived in India for thousands of years, their cuisine, influenced by local flavours, has remained distinctive. The Sindhis are another example of a community which came to India after the Partition. Their cuisine, yummy and delicious, has found a pride of place in India. Similarly, the Marwari cuisine from Rajasthan has become known for its delicate flavours and elegance of service. Bengal too has a host of food ideas to offer to an enthusiastic hostess.

Here I have chosen four sample ethnic theme parties. The table decor, the atmosphere, the peripheral salads, chutneys and pickles can be designed to suit the main theme. I hope the four menu ideas serve as an inspiration to delve into the treasure box of Indian cuisine and explore its unlimited possibilities.

Bengali

menu

dahiwala korma
jhinga matar ki curry
machchli ka pulao
ande palakwale
munakkewali chane ki dal
bhaja begun
radha ballavi
patisapta

Rajasthani

menu

gatta pulao
kanji achar
dal ki roti
aam ki launji
aloo ki bhooni khichree
dahiwale thareya
gulgulle malaiwale

Parsi

menu

dhan sak
khatte mithe baingan
pyazwale chawal
jhinge ka patia
gosht bhuna tamater ke saucewala
mava almond pudding
lagan nu custard

Sindhi

menu

sayel gosht
sabziyonki sindhi kadhi
sagwali macaroni
sadhe chawal
missi roti
chawal aur boondi ki kheer
sev ki barfi

DAHIWALA KORMA

(Mutton in Yoghurt)

Serves: 6 **Cooking Time: 1 hr 30 mins**

1 kg. mutton, cubed
1 cup yoghurt
3 onions, ground
1 tsp. ginger-garlic paste
2 bay leaves
1 tsp. sugar
1 tsp. whole garam masala (cloves, cardamom, cinnamon peppercorns)
Ghee
Salt to taste

Add ground ginger-garlic paste to the curd and beat well. Marinate meat in the curd for 1 hour. Heat a pressure cooker and add 5 tbsp. ghee. Add ground onion and bay leaves and the masalas. Fry for a few seconds. Add the marinated meat and simmer slowly till cooked. Add salt to taste and simmer. Do not add water. If required, just sprinkle a little water towards the end. Serve hot with a trickle of ghee poured over the korma and sliced onions.

JHINGA MATAR KI CURRY

(Pea and Prawn Curry)

Serves: 6 **Cooking Time: 1 hr 30 mins**

1/2 kg. medium-sized prawns shelled, deveined
1 1/2 cup shelled peas
Oil as needed
Salt to taste

Grind for masala I:
2.5 cm. cinnamon
2 bay leaves
2 cloves

1/4 cup curd, beaten
1 cup coconut milk
3/4 tsp. *sugar*

Grind for masala II:
2 onions
2.5 cm. ginger
2 red chillies
1 tsp. turmeric and corianader powder

Apply turmeric and salt to the deveined prawns and keep aside. After ten minutes, fry them in oil lightly and remove. Heat 2 tbsp. oil and fry ground masala I till brown. Add the peas and sugar and salt to taste. Fry for a while. Add masala II. Cover and cook till peas are tender. Then add the prawns and cook till soft. Put in the well-beaten curd. Cook for 2 minutes and add the coconut milk. Cook till the gravy is thick and creamy.

MACHCHLI KA PULAO

(Fish Pulao)

Serves: 6 **Cooking Time: 1 hr**

500 gm. pomfrets, filleted
1 medium onion, chopped
1 tsp. turmerci powder
4 red chillies
1 1/2 cup rice
2 tbsp. ghee
11/2 tsp. garam masala powder
1 tbsp. lemon juice
1 small bunch coriander leaves, chopped
Oil as needed
Salt to taste

Wash and dry the fish and cut into pieces. Heat 1 tbsp. oil. Add turmeric, chopped coriander, chillies, garam masala and salt to taste. let it sizzle for 2–3 minutes. Then add the lemon juice and put in the pieces of fish and fry them well on both sides so that the masala coats them well. When they are cooked, remove and reserve. Fry the chopped onion to a light brown, add the rice and salt and fry for 2–3 minutes. Add 3 cups of hot water and cook till nearly done. Then place fish pieces on top and cover. Cook on a very low heat. Let the rice cook till all water evaporates. Serve hot.

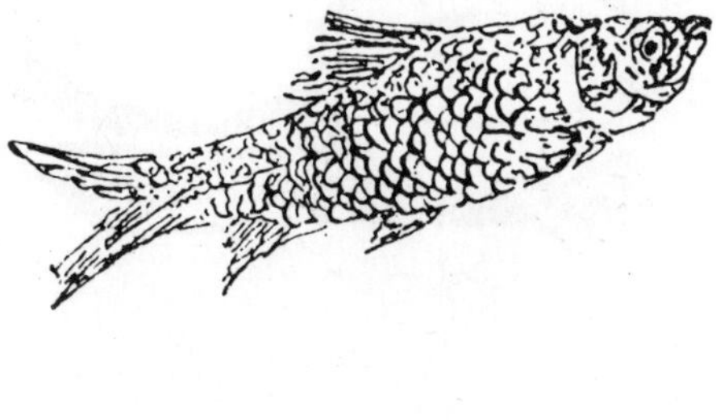

ANDE PALAKWALE

(Fried Egg Quarters on Spinach)

Serves: 6 **Cooking Time: 1 hr 30 minutes**

1/4 kg. spinach
2 onions, chopped finely
4 hard boiled eggs, peeled
1 egg, beaten
1 cup breadcrumbs
1 tbsp. seasoned flour
Oil for frying
Salt and pepper to taste

Chop spinach finely and cook in enough water till tender. Heat 1 tbsp. oil and fry the onions till golden brown. Season with salt and pepper. Add spinach *puree.* Cook till thick. Roll the eggs in seasoned flour, coat with beaten egg and breadcrumbs. Fry in hot oil until golden brown in colour. Cut each egg into four. Serve the spinach mixture, garnished with egg-quarters.

MUNAKKEWALI CHANE KI DAL

(Raisin Chana Dal)

Serves: 6 **Cooking Time: 1 hr 45 mins**

1 cup Bengal gram (chana dal), soaked in water for 2 hours
1/2 coconut, cut into small pieces 10 raisins
$^{2}/_{3}$ green chillies
Oil as needed
Salt to taste

For garam masala:
2 bay leaves
1 tsp. ground red chillies
2.5 cm. ginger
1 tsp. cumin seed powder

Boil dal with salt till tender. Each grain of the dal must be soft and separate. Heat oil. Add the garam masala and pour over the dal. Fry small cubes of coconut and put in dal. Add the raisins and 2–3 slit green chillies. Simmer till well done. Serve with *puris.*

BHAJA BEGUN

(Fried Brinjals)

Serves: 6

Cooking Time: 1 hr

500 gm, round small brinials
Oil for frying

For grinding:
11/2 tsp. coriander powder
1 tsp. chilli powder
2 green chillies
1/2 tsp. turmeric powder
2 cm. piece ginger
1/2 tsp. sugar
Salt to taste

Cut the brinjals into 1 cm. round slices. Apply the ground masala on both sides and fry in hot oil to a golden brown. Serve hot with a little mint chutney on top.

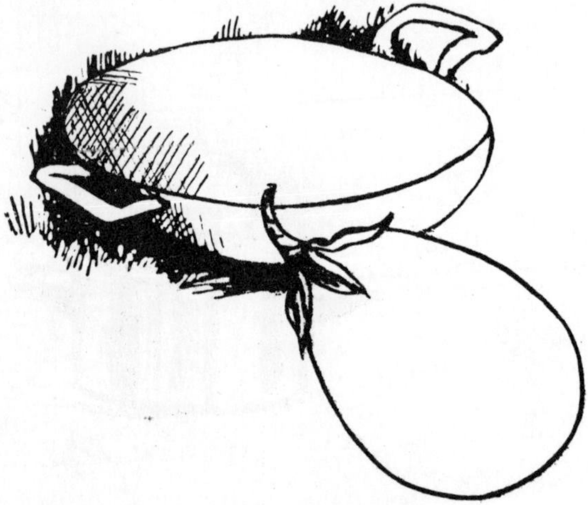

RADHA BALLAVI

(Dal Rotis)

Serves: 6

Cooking Time: 1 hr

1/4 kg. *chana dal*
1/2 kg. flour (*maida*)
Oil for frying
Salt to taste

For grinding:
2.5 cm. ginger
1 tsp. garam masala powder
1 tsp. chilli powder
1 tsp. cumin seeds

Knead the flour into a dough with enough oil, salt and water. Boil the dal with salt. Mash completely into a dry paste and add the ground masala and ground ginger. Cover small balls of the dal mixture with dough and roll carefully into *rotis*. Fry on a griddle smearing oil on both sides keeping the *rotis* soft.

PATISAPTA

(Semolina Dessert)

Serves: 6 **Cooking Time: 1 hr 30 mins**

For batter:
1 cup semolina
1 cup wholewheat flour (*atta*)
1 cup cream
1 tbsp. oil
A little milk (optional)

For filling:
1 cup jaggery
1 coconut, grated
1 cup khoya

Mix jaggery, coconut and *khoya* and cook on a low fire till the mixture leaves the sides of the vessel. Reserve.

Mix semolina, *atta,* and oil to make a smooth batter with water or milk. Heat a griddle and smear a little oil on it. When the oil smokes, pour a ladle of batter on it and spread it thinly with the ladle in a round shape. Put some filling on the cooked round and roll it and remove to a plate. Prepare all the pancakes in the same way. Serve with cream.

GATTHA PULAO

(Dumpling Rice)

Serves: 6 **Cooking Times: 1 hr**

$1^1/_2$ cups *basmati* rice, soaked in water for 2 hours
1 cup gram flour (*besan*)
$1^1/_2$ tsp. chilli powder
$^1/_2$ tsp. turmeric powder
1 tsp. garam masala powder
$^1/_2$ cup raisins, soaked in water, drained
5 tbsp. ghee
1 tsp. cumin seeds
$^1/_4$ tsp. asafoetida
Salt to taste

Drain rice. Cook in fresh water ($3^1/_2$ cups) till done. Drain out all water. Reserve rice. Knead a dough with besan, $^1/_2$ tsp. cumin seeds, $^1/_2$ tsp. garam masala, $^1/_2$ tsp. chilli powder, 1 tbsp. ghee, a little turmeric and salt, adding water. Knead and roll in cylindrical shapes—8 in all, 2 cm. in diameter. Boil water in a large pan and as it simmers, put the rolls in it. Cook till the rolls are done and white in colour. Drain and reserve the *gatthas.*

Heat remaining ghee. Add cumin seeds, asafoetida and the sliced *gatthas.* Add raisins and Stir. Add all remaining spices and the cooked rice. Mix well and heat through. Serve hot.

KANJI ACHAR

(Carrot Pickle)

Serves: 6 **Cooking Time: 15 mins**

6 carrots, peeled, cut in slices or sticks
3 tsp. mustard seeds, ground
2 tsp. chilli powder
1/2 tsp. turmeric powder
2 tsp. salt

Mix all ingredients in 5 cups of water or more as needed. Keep in the sun for 3 to 4 days. Use when carrots are soft.

• • •

DAL KI ROTI

(Lentil Rotis)

Serves: 6 **Cooking Times: 1 hr**

1 cup green gram dal (*moong dal*) ground
2 cup wholemeal flour (*atta*)
1 tsp. chilli powder
1 tsp. garam masala powder
1/2 tsp. corinander powder
Ghee
Salt to taste

Knead all ingredients using 2 tbsp. ghee and enough water to make a stiff dough. Make small lemon-sized balls and roll out into *rotis.* Cook on a griddle, smearing with ghee on both sides. Serve hot.

AAM KI LAUNJI

(Mango Savoury)

Serves: 6 **Cooking Time: 30 mins**

3 ripe mangoes, sliced into strips with skin
$^1/_2$ tsp. turmeric
$^1/_2$ tsp. coriander powder
1 tsp. chilli powder
$^1/_4$ tsp. fenugreek seeds
$^1/_2$ tsp. cumin seeds
$^1/_2$ tsp. aniseed
$^1/_2$ tsp. mustard seeds
$^3/_4$ cup sugar
A pinch of asafoetida
Ghee

Heat 2 tbsp. ghee. Fry cumin seeds, aniseed, mustard and asafoetida. Then add the mango slices. Add other dry ingredients. Cook for a few minutes. Add sugar and $1^1/_2$ cups water. Cook on medium heat till well blended and thick. Serve with rice or *chappatis.*

ALOO KI BHOONI KHICHREE

(Potato Savoury)

Serves: 6 **Cooking Time: 45 mins**

5 large potatoes
2 tbsp. roasted peauts, ground
$^1/_2$ tsp. cumin seeds
1 green chilli, cut finely
1 tsp. sugar
2 tbsp. grated coconut
2 tbsp. coriander leaves, chopped
2 tbsp. ghee
Salt to taste

Grate the potatoes with their skin and wash well. Heat ghee. Add cumin seeds and other masalas except for coriander and coconut. Put in the potatoes and cook covered for 10 minutes on a slow fire till tender. Sprinkle with coconut and corinder and serve hot.

DAHIWALE THAREYA

(Moong Dal Pakoras in Curd)

Serves: 6 **Cooking Time: 1 hr**

2 cups *moong dal* soaked in water for 3 hours
4 green chillies
2 cm. piece ginger
1 tsp. chilli powder
3 cups curd, beaten
A small bunch coriander leaves, chopped
Oil
Salt to taste

Wash and grind dal to a smooth paste with green chillies, ginger and 1 tsp. chilli powder. Add salt to taste and coriander leaves. Mix well but do not beat. Heat oil in a pan. Take a stainless sieve with big holes and press the dal down into the sieve with the hand quickly. Let the drops fall into the hot oil. Make them crisp and golden brown. Dip in water for a minutes and add to curd. Finally decorate curd with a sprinkling of chilli powder or cumin seed powder.

GULGULLE MALAIWALE

(Sweet Dumplings with Cream)

Serves: 6 **Cooking Time: 1 hr**

$^1/_2$ cup flour (*maida*)
$^1/_2$ cup wholemeal flour (*atta*)
$^3/_4$ cup sugar
2 tbsp. jaggery
5 green cardamoms, crushed
1 cup cream
$^1/_2$ tsp. aniseed, crushed
$^1/_4$ tsp. peppercorns, crushed
1 cup milk
A pinch of soda bi carb
Ghee

Mix the sugar and jaggery in the milk and boil it till well dissolved. Mix all the other ingredients except for the ghee with flour and *atta*. Now pour the milk in this mixture and form a thick soft dough. Heat ghee, make small balls from the dough and fry to a golden brown in the ghee. Serve hot with cream.

DHAN SAK

(Dal)

Serves: 6 **Cooking Time: 1 hr 30 mins**

$^1/_2$ kg. mutton
8 tbsp. *tuvar* dal
2 tsp. *masur* dal
1 big piece red pumkin
2 small potatoes
4 small tomatoes
2 medium-sized onion
2 green chillies
$^1/_2$ tsp. turmeric powder
1 onion, chopped finely
1 bunch *methi* leaves, chopped
2 brinjals

To be ground:
$1^1/_2$ tsp. cumin seeds
2 tsp. coriander seeds
2.5 cm. piece ginger
2 red chillies
4 cloves garlic
2 tbsp. vinegar

Clean and cut the mutton into square pieces. Heat a pressure cooker and add the mutton, dals, vegetables cut into fairly large pieces, salt, chillies and turmeric. Cook till meat and dals are soft. Remove the cooker and take out the meat pieces. Mash the dals and vegetables well till smooth.

Heat a pan and add 2 tbsp. oil. Add the chopped onion and ground ingredients. Fry till pink in colour. Add the meat and fry well. Add the mashed vegetables and dals. Reduce the heat and simmer on a slow fire. Serve after adding a little lime juice.

KHATTE MITHE BAINGAN

(Sweet and Sour Brinjals)

Serves: 6 **Cooking Time: 1 hr**

10 small round brinjals
2 tbsp. vinegar
1 tbsp. brown sugar
1 tsp. raisins, chopped
Salt to taste
Oil

To Grind:
2 medium sized onions
2.5 cm. piece ginger
4 cloves garlic
2 green chillies
1 tsp. mustard seeds
$^1/_2$ tsp. turmeric powder
$^1/_2$ tsp. chilli powder
$^1/_4$ coconut, grated

Wash brinjals and slit them into four without cutting them apart. Keep aside. Heat a *kerai* on fire and add 3 tbsp. oil. Fry the ground masala paste to a golden colour. Remove. In the same *kerai,* add the raisins and fry for a second. Remove. Stuff this mixture adding salt inside the slit brinjals. Arrange all the stuffed brinjals in a shallow pan. Sprinkle a little water and oil over them. Cover and cook till brinjals are tender. Add sugar and vinegar and simmer for a few minutes. Serve hot.

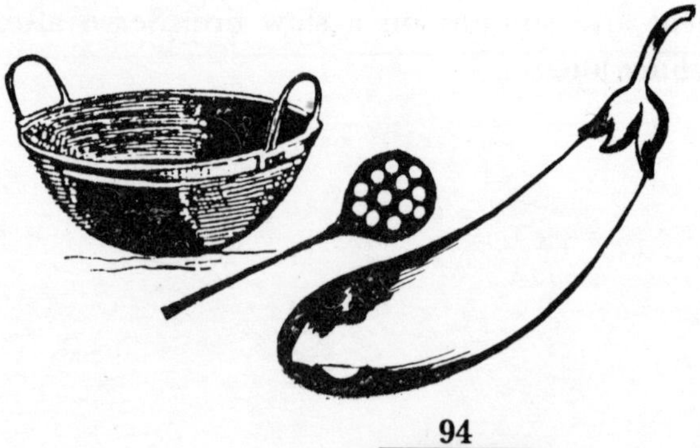

PYAZWALE CHAWAL

(Brown Rice with Onion)

Serves: 6 **Cooking Time: 1 hr**

1 cup rice
2 small onions, sliced finely
1 big piece cinnamon
2 bay leaves
2 cloves
2 white cardamoms
2 peppercorns
1 tbsp. sugar
$^1/_2$ tsp. cumin seeds
Oil
Salt to taste

Soak rice for 1 hour. Mix the sugar with 3 tbsp. water and cook on low fire till it is a rich brown in colour. Add two cups of water to it. Remove from fire.

Heat oil and fry the onions till golden in colour. Add the rice. Fry for a while. Add the brown sugar water, all whole masalas, and salt. Cover and cook on a very low fire till soft.

JHINGE KA PATIA

(Prawn Patia)

Serves: 6 **Cooking Time: 1 hr**

3 cups shelled, deveined prawns
2 large onions, chopped finely
$^1/_4$ coconut, grated
5 red chillies
6 cloves garlic
1 tsp. cumin seeds
$^1/_2$ tsp. Turmeric powder
$^1/_2$ tsp. chilli powder
2 large tomatoes, chopped
$^1/_2$ tsp. coriander-cumin powder
$^1/_2$ tsp. curry powder
2 tbsp. jaggery
1 tsp. lemon juice
Oil as needed
Salt to taste

Grind coconut, cumin seeds, garlic and red chillies to a paste. Heat 2 tbsp. oil in a *kerai.* Fry the onion till brown. Add the ground paste and fry on slow fire. Add turmeric powder, chilli powder, coriander-cumin powder. Fry for a while. Add the deveined shelled prawns. Add chopped tomatoes. Do not add water. Let the prawns cook on a slow fire, keeping some water on the lid. When prawns are cooked, add grated jaggery and lime juice to taste. Serve hot.

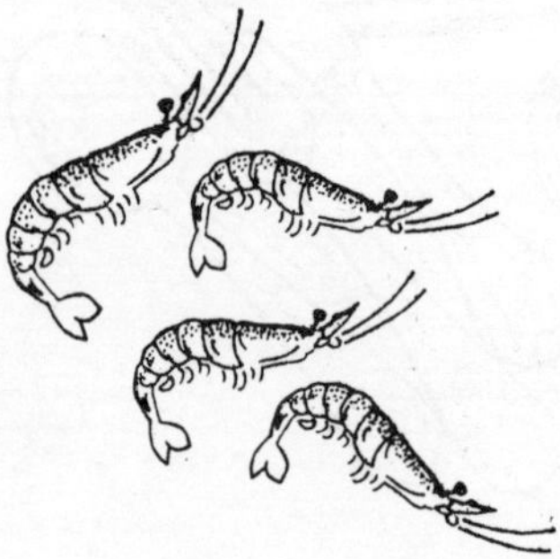

GOSHT BHUNA TAMATER KE SAUCEWALA

(Mutton in Tomato Sauce)

Serves: 6 **Cooking Time: 1 hr**

$^{1}/_{2}$ kg. mutton, cut into pieces
$^{1}/_{2}$ kg. red tomatoes
$1^{1}/_{2}$ tbsp. butter
2 tbsp. flour
$1^{1}/_{2}$ tsp. sugar
Salt to taste

For Grinding:
2 medium onions
4 green chillies
2.5 cm. ginger
2 cloves garlic

Mix 1 tbsp. flour, salt and pepper to a paste. Apply this to the mutton pieces and cook in hot oil. Remove from oil. Boil the tomatoes, remove the skin and mash them well. Heat the butter, add the flour, stir, then add the ground masalas. Cook for a few minutes and add the mashed tomatoes. Add the sugar and salt and cook till sauce is thick and creamy. Add the meat pieces and simmer. Serve hot.

MAVA ALMOND PUDDING

(Badam Pak)

Serves: 6 **Cooking Time: 1 hr 30 mins**

500 gm. almonds
500 gm. *mava*
500 gm. sugar
$1^1/_2$ cup ghee
10 cardamoms
1 grated nutmeg
2 cup pure ghee

Heat $^1/_2$ the ghee, sugar and water on a low fire till sugar melts. Increase the heat slowly and let the syrup boil for a few minutes. Add the remaining ghee and *mava* gradually stirring constantly. Add sliced almonds and pure ghee. Continue cooking till the mixture leaves the sides of the vessel. Remove from fire, add powdered cardamom and nutmeg when slightly cool. Spread on a greased *thali* and cut into squares.

LAGAN NU CUSTARD

(Baked Custard)

Serves: 6 **Cooking Time: 1 hr**

1.5 litres milk
400 gm. cream
Sugar to taste
1 tbsp. almonds, *charoli*, cashewnuts
$^1/_4$ cup rose water
$^1/_2$ tsp. ground cardamom, nutmeg

Boil 1 litre milk with sugar until it becomes almost half the original quantity. Cool. Beat 5 yolks and 3 egg whites. Add cream, $^1/_2$ litre milk and rose water and nuts to it. Blend well with thickened milk. Put in ground spices.

Grease a baking dish and pour the mixture into it. Bake in a hot oven in a tray of water for $^1/_2$ an hour or till set. Cool and cut into slices.

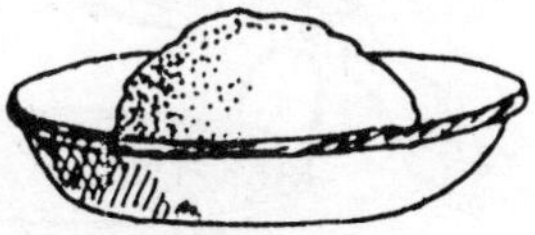

SAYEL GOSHT

(Fried Mutton)

Serves: 6 **Cooking Time: 1 hr**

$^1/_2$ kg. mutton
$^1/_2$ cup coriander, chopped
2 tbsp. mint leaves, chopped
3 tbsp. ghee
2 tbsp. coriander powder
3 large tomatoes, chopped
$^1/_4$ kg. onions, chopped
$^1/_2$ tsp. chilli/turmeric powder
2 tbsp. curd
Salt to taste

Mix all the ingredients in bowl. Heat ghee in a *dekchi* and fry the mixed ingredients. Cover with a lid and seal the edges with a little dough. Now simmer the mutton till tender on a slow fire.

SABZIYON KI SINDHI KADHI

(Mixed Vegetable Curry)

Serves: 6 **Cooking Time: 1 hr 15 mins**

1 cup chopped vegetable *guvar* (cluster beans) *bendi* (lady fingers), beans, drum sticks, potatoes
1 tbsp. gram flour (besan)
1/2 tsp. mustard seeds
1/2 tsp. fenugreek seeds
1/4 tsp. cumin seeds a pinch of turmeric powder
1 tbsp. tamarind water
8 curry leaves
1/4 tsp. ginger, chopped
Oil
Salt to taste

Heat oil and fry the mustard, fenugreek and cumin seeds. When they splutter, add *besan* and cook on a very slow fire till slightly brown. Add water according the amount of gram flour used and add the chopped vegetables. Add salt to taste, turmeric powder, curry leaves and ginger. Cook till vegetables are tender. Add a little tamarind water and let it simmer. Garnish with coriander leaves and serve with rice.

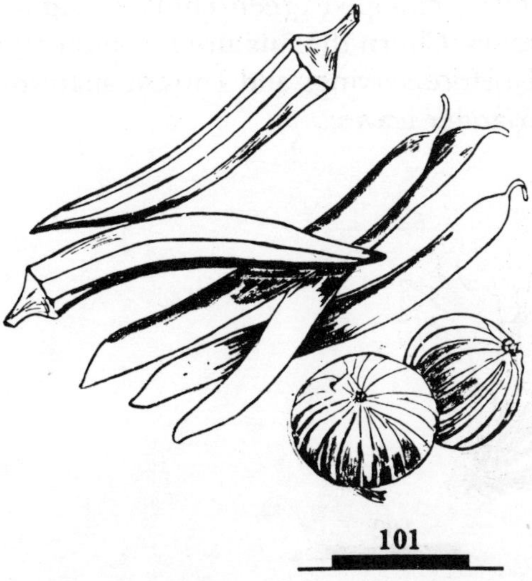

SAGWALI MACARONI

(Macaroni In Spinach)

Serves: 6 **Cooking Time: 1 hr**

4 bunches spinach
2 bunches *methi* (fenugreek)
1 bunch *suva* (fennel leaves)
1 bunch *khatta palak*
1 brinial
100 gm. white pumpkin
2 carrots
2 onions
250 gm. macaroni
3 tomatoes
50 gm. cluster beans (Gurar)
2.5 cm. ginger
6 cloves garlic
6 green chillies
1/2 tsp. chilli/turmeric powder
1 tsp. coriander/cumin powder
2 tbsp. corinader leaves, chopped
1/2 cup *chana dal*, soaked in water
Oil
Salt to taste

Boil macaroni in salted water. Strain and keep aside. In a pressure cooker and a tbsp. of oil. Fry garlic and ginger ground to paste. Add all cleaned and chopped vegetables. Clean and chop all leafy vegetables finely. Add to the vegetables. Cook for a while. Add the drained *chana dal*. Add the dry masala powders, chopped green chillies. Add salt and cook for 25 minutes. Churn the mixture to a paste. Just one cup water and before serving, add cooked macaroni and garnish with coriander leaves.

SADHE CHAWAL

(Plain Rice)

Serves: 6 **Cooking Time: 30 mins**

3 cups rice
1 tsp. cumin seeds
2 tsp. oil
Salt to taste

Clean rice. In a pressure cooker fry the cumin seeds. Add the rice. Fry for a few minutes. Add 3 to 4 cups hot water and salt. Pressure cook till 3 whistles. Remove and cool.

• • •

MISSI ROTI

(Gram Flour Chappatis)

Serves: 6 **Cooking Time: 1 hr 15 mins**

$^1/_2$ kg. gram flour
3 medium onions, chopped
2 green chillies, chopped
3 cloves garlic
3 tsp. pomegranate seeds, ground
2 tbsp. curd
$^1/_2$ tsp. chilli powder
10 mint leaves, chopped
1 tbsp. coriander leaves, chopped
2 tbsp. ghee
Salt to taste

Mix all the ingredients. Add curd and water to form a stiff dough. Leave aside for 30 minutes. Roll into *chapatis* and cook on medium heat.

CHAWAL AUR BOONDI KI KHEER

(Rice and Boondi Pudding)

Serves: 6

Cooking Time: 1 hr

$^1/_2$ cup rice
$^1/_2$ cup *boondi*
2 litre milk

1 cup sugar
1 tbsp. cashew/almonds, broken
1 tsp. cardamom powder

Cook the rice in milk till soft. Add sugar and cook till well blended. Add fried nuts and cardamom powder. At the time of serving, sprinkle the *boondi* over and serve.

• • •

SEV KI BARFI

(Semolina Squares)

Serves: 6

Cooking Time: 1 hr

500 gm. ready made *sev* without salt
250 gm. sugar
150 gm. ghee

1 tbsp. fried nuts
1 tsp. cardamom powder
Silver *varkh*

Cook the *sev* in just sufficient water. Add the sugar and cook till the *sev* is blended well and the mixture leaves the sides of the vessel. While stirring, add the ghee and exhaust the same before removing the mixture from the vessel. Add the cardamom powder. Pour the mixture onto a greased *thali*. Level. Decorate with fried nuts and spread the silver *varkh*. Cool. Cut into desired shapes.

festival parties

The joyful spirit of India's people is reflected in the celebration of its colourful festivals. Being a predominantly agricultural country, India depends largely on the monsoon for its prosperity and plenty. Naturally, most of the major festivals of the country come during the four monsoon months when fields are verdant and cascading rivers bring life to the landscape. When the rice saplings are shooting up, when corn cobs are just beginning to hold pearly grains together, it is time for the farmer to take time off till the harvesting is ready to be done. So there is a great deal of merriment, dancing, singing, celebrating and of course, eating. Among the other festivals which mean extra special food are *Janmashtami* or the birthday of lord *Krishna, Dussera* or *Devi Puja* and *Diwali* the festival of lights. *Holi,* a colourful festival is a harbinger of spring.

In the following menus, I have made an effort to capture the generosity with which food is served on festive days. The festive cuisine of India is also noteworthy for its simplicity because it is mostly vegetarian and uncomplicated in nature. Four festivals and their slightly unusual, non-traditional fare has been highlighted in these menus. The dishes can be interchanged or combinations can be made to suit personal tastes.

Holi

menu–I

badami doodh
chirotee
surnoli
kadamb
doodh ki roti (dashami)
meweki usal
aloo moongfali
moong dal atwal
keleki puri

Janmashtmi

menu–II

giri ki kheer
prabhu bhog ke chawal
aloo ki tilwai tiki
dahi ki chutney
rassedar aloo
bahurangi puris
elaichi kalakand
shahed khajoor ki karanji

Dussera

menu–III

arbi patteka saag
methiya dal
pithi poori
kesariya biryani
kachche aam ki chutney
bhaja aloo
aam aur keleka rasayan

Diwali

menu–IV

mirchi pohe usal
vatana karanjis
badam ki barfi
besan ki mithai
aloo saunf ki puri
seb ki chutney
rajali keleki mithi poli
aam ka mitha

BADAMI DOODH

(Almond Milk)

Serves: 6 **Cooking Time: 1 hr**

$1^1/_2$ litre milk
$^1/_4$ cup almonds, soaked in water
$^1/_2$ cup sugar or to taste
$^1/_2$ cup cream
$^1/_2$ tsp. cardamom powder
$^1/_2$ tsp. saffron, soaked in 1 tsp. milk

Peel the almonds and grind to a fine paste. Cook in the milk till blended. Add sugar. Cook further for 5 minutes. Add saffron and cardamom powder. Simmer and remove. Cool and refrigerate. Serve cold in glasses topped with a blob of cream.

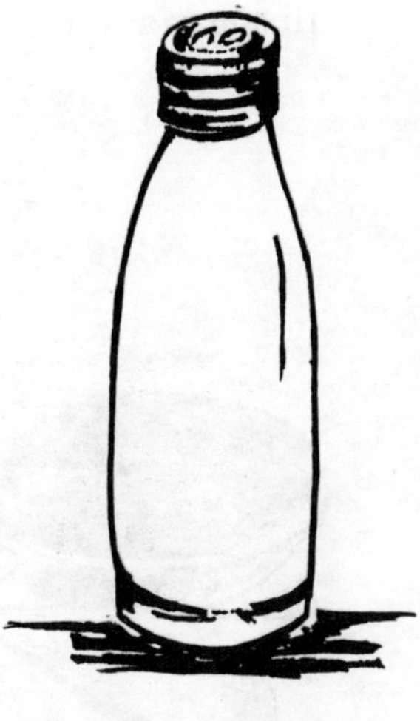

CHIROTEE

(Sweet Flaky Biscuits)

Serves: 6 **Cooking Time: 1 hr**

2 cups flour (*maida*)
2 tbsp. ghee
A pinch of salt
2 tbsp. rice flour
2 tbsp. ghee, melted
$^1/_2$ cup ground sugar
$^1/_2$ tsp. cardamom powder
Ghee for frying

Knead a stiff dough with flour, ghee and water, adding salt. Mix rice flour and ghee. Reserve. Roll out nine thin *chapatis* of the dough. Make sets of three each thus: Put one *chapati* flat on a board. Smear with rice and ghee mixture. Repeat so that there are three sets of three each. Roll each set. Cut into slices 1 cm wide. Roll out each slice again to a 5 cm. disc, keeping the cut side on top. Fry five or six discs at a time till golden. Drain on absorbent paper. Sprinkle with sugar and cardamom powder.

SURNOLI

(Sweet Sour Pancakes)

Serves: 6 **Cooking Time: 1 hr 30 mins**

1 cup rice, soaked in water for 3 hours, drained
3/4 cup *pohe* (flaked rice) soaked in 1/2 cup buttermilk for 1/2 hour
3/4 cup grated coconut
1/2 cup grated jaggery
1/2 tsp. turmeric powder
Ghee as needed
A pinch of salt

Grind all ingredients, adding rice, jaggery and salt last of all. The batter should be thick. Keep overnight. On a greased griddle, spread a large spoonful. Cover with a lid.

Cook on a low flame. When cooked, lift carefully to a plate.

Surnolis are cooked only on one side. The top side should be light and spongy. Serve with melted homemade ghee.

KADAMB

(Pumpkin Cake)

Serves: 6 **Cooking Time: 1 hr**

1/2 kg. red pumpkin, peeled, grated
2 cups rice semolina
1/2 cup grated coconut
1/2 cup grated jaggery
1/2 tsp. cardamom powder
1/2 tsp. salt
Ghee as needed.

Mix coconut and jaggery. Add grated pumpkin. Add salt and rice semolina. Add cardamom powder.

Fill this mixture in greased bowls and steam cook for 1/2 an hour. Remove and serve hot with melted homemade ghee.

• • •

DOODH KI ROTI (DASHAMI)

(Milk Rotis)

Serves: 8 **Cooking Time: 1 hr**

4 cups wholemeal flour (*atta*) sieved
1 cup milk
Salt to taste

Knead flour with milk, adding salt to taste. Add enough milk to make a soft dough. Make lemon-sized balls and roll out into 16 cm. discs. Dry roast on both sides on a griddle and serve hot with ghee.

MEWE KI USAL

(Dry Fruit Sweet)

Serves: 6 **Cooking Time: 1 hr**

1 cup cashewnuts
1 cup peanuts
10 almonds
5 walnuts
$^1/_2$ cup raisins
8 dried apricots,seeded (soaked for 3 hours in water)
1 tbsp. honey
2 tbsp. ghee
1 tsp. lemon juice
$^1/_2$ tsp. ginger juice

Drain all dry fruits and nuts. Heat ghee. Add all nuts and dry fruits. Stir fry till coated with ghee and pink in colour, sprinkling milk if needed. Add honey, lemon and ginger juice. Serve hot or cold.

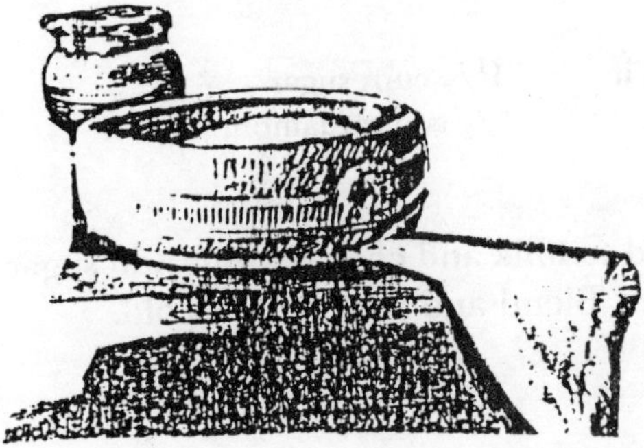

ALOO MOONGFALI

(Potatoes and Peanuts)

Serves: 6 **Cooking Time: 45 mins**

4 large potatoes, boiled, peeled, cubed
$^1/_2$ cup peanuts, roasted coarsely pounded
3 green chillies, chopped
5 curry leaves
$^1/_2$ tsp. cumin seeds
4 tbsp. ghee
1 tbsp. lemon juice
1 tbsp. sugar
Salt to taste

Heat ghee. Add cumin seed, curry leaves. When seeds pop, add chillies, potatoes and peanuts. Stir till pinkish brown. Add sugar, salt and lemon juice. Serve with *puris.*

•••

MOONG DAL ATWAL

(Lentil Sweet)

Serves: 6 **Cooking Time: 45 mins**

1 cup *moong dal,* soaked in water for $^1/_2$ an hour
5 cups milk
$1^1/_2$ cups sugar
$^1/_2$ tsp. cardamom powder

Drain dal and add to milk and cook till soft. Add sugar and cardamom powder. Blend and serve hot or cold.

KELE KI PURI

(Banana Puris)

Serves: 6 **Cooking Time: 1 hr**

3 cups wholewheat flour (*atta*) sieved
3 bananas
$^3/_4$ cup milk
$^1/_4$ tsp. salt
Ghee for frying

Knead a firm dough with all the ingredients except ghee. Make small balls and roll out each to 8 cm discs. Deep fry in hot ghee till puffed and golden. Boiled, peeled and mashed sweet potatoes can be used instead of bananas.

GIRI KI KHEER

(Almond Kheer)

Serves: 6 **Cooking Time: 1 hr**

- $^1/_2$ cup rice, soaked in water, drained, dried
- 1 tin sweetened condensed milk
- 2 cups milk
- $^1/_2$ cup almond powder
- 4 *pedhas*
- 2 tbsp. pistachios, minced
- 2 tbsp. raisins
- 1 tsp. cardamom powder
- $^1/_2$ tsp. saffron
- Sugar as needed

Grind rice to a rough semolina-like powder. Add 4 cups water and boil till done—there should be no lumps. Add sweetened milk, plain milk and almond powder mixed with a little water. Blend well and cook. If needed, add more sugar. Add cardamom powder, saffron, raisins and nuts. Add crushed *pedhas* and simmer till fragrant and creamy. Add milk if needed. Chill and serve.

PRABHU BHOG KE CHAWAL

(Yoghurt Nut Rice)

Serves: 6 **Cooking Time: 30 mins**

3 cups rice, cooked
6 cups fresh yoghurt
1 cup savoury *boondi* drops
$^1/_2$ cup cashewnuts, stir-fried
$^1/_4$ cup raisins, soaked in water drained
$^1/_4$ cup walnuts, pounded coarsely
2 green chillies, minced
5 curry leaves
1 cup coriander leaves,minced
$^1/_2$ tsp. cumin seeds
2 tsp. oil
2 tsp. sugar
Salt to taste

Mix all ingredients except oil,boondis, cumin seeds and curry leaves. Chill. Heat oil. Add cumin seeds and curry leaves. When seeds pop pour over rice. Chill and serve adding boondis on top.

ALOO KI TILWALI TIKI

(Potato Sesame Packs)

Serves: 6 **Cooking Time: 1 hr**

8 potatoes, boiled, peeled, mashed
4 slices of bread, soaked in a little milk, mashed
1 tsp. *anardana*, pounded
1 tsp. *amchur* (mango powder)
1 tsp. mint leaves, minced
2 tbsp. coriander leaves, minced
$^1/_2$ cup cashewnuts, pounded coarsely
1 cup sesame seeds
Oil for frying

Mix and knead all ingredients well except sesame seeds and oil. Form into small rolls and dip or roll over in sesame seeds. Deep fry till golden. Drain on absorbent paper and serve with dahi ki chutney.

• • •

DAHI KI CHUTNEY

(Yoghurt Chutney)

Serves: 6 **Cooking Time: 15 mins**

$^1/_2$ cup yoghurt, beaten
1 cup coriander leaves, chopped
2 green chillies
1 tsp. grated ginger
Salt and sugar to taste

Grind all the ingredients except yoghurt to a fine paste. Mix with yoghurt and chill.

RASSEDAR ALOO

(Potatoes in Ginger Gravy)

Serves: 6 **Cooking Time: 30 mins**

6 potatoes, boiled, peeled, cubed
1 green chilli, chopped
1 tsp. chilli powder
1 tsp. dried ginger powder
$^1/_2$ tsp. turmeric powder
2 cups coriander leaves, chopped
1 tsp. *amchur* powder
$^1/_2$ tsp. cumin seeds
$^1/_4$ cup oil
Salt and sugar to taste

Heat oil. Add cumin seeds. When they pop, add potatoes and all other ingredients. Stir. Add 2 $^1/_2$ cups water and simmer till gravy is thick. Serve with *puris*.

• • •

BAHURANGI PURIS

(Colourful Puris)

Serves: 6 **Cooking Time: 1 hr**

3 cups wholemeal flour (*atta*)
2 tbsp. oil
1 drop of yellow colour
1 drop of pink colour
Oil for deep frying
Salt to taste

Add oil and salt to sieved flour. Add water to knead a stiff dough. To one third share, add yellow colour and knead. To another one third, add pink colour and knead. Now roll all dough together and make into small balls. Roll out into 8 cm discs and deep fry till puffed and golden. Serve with potato gravy.

ELAICHI KALAKAND

(Milk Pudding)

Serves: 6 **Cooking Time: 1 hr**

2 litres milk
2 grains of tartaric acid
$1^1/_2$ cup sugar
1 tsp. cardamom powder
Leaves of silver *varkh*
2 tbsp. pistachios, minced

Heat milk till creamy. Add sugar and the tartaric acid. Add cardamom powder and pistachios, leaving some for garnishing. Cook till thick and creamy. Pour into a plate. Cool. Decorate with nuts and silver *varkh* and cut into squares.

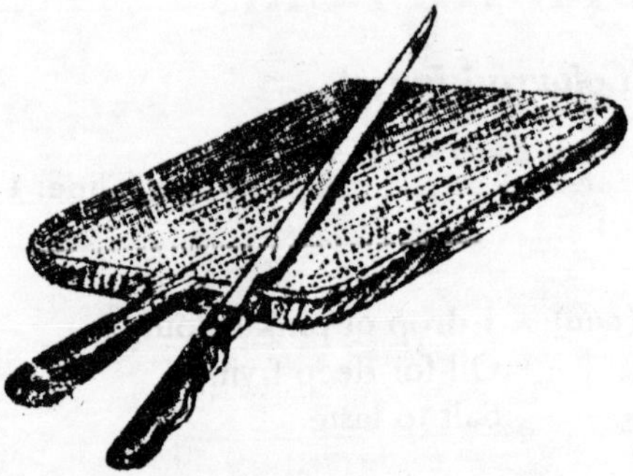

SHAHED KHAJOOR KI KARANJI

(Honey Date Packets)

Serves: 6 **Cooking Time: 1 hr**

2 cup refined flour
$^1/_4$ cup semolina
$^1/_2$ tsp. baking powder
4 tbsp. ghee
1 pinch of salt
Oil or ghee for frying

For filling:
$^1/_4$ cup honey
1 cup dates, seeded
$^1/_2$ cup almonds, pounded
1 tsp. cardamom powder

Grind the filling into a paste. Reserve. Make a stiff dough with all other ingredients except ghee or oil for frying. Divide dough into small balls and roll out each to 8 cm disc. Put a spoon of filling in the centre and fold over. Flute the edges to make a half moonshape. Make all karanjis and leave to dry on a piece of muslin. Deep fry in batches till golden and crisp.

ARBI PATTE KA SAAG

(Colocacia Leaves in Gravy)

Serves: 6 **Cooking Time: 1 hr**

- 2 bunches tender *arvi* leaves chopped, stems, peeled and chopped
- 1 bunch *khata palak* leaves, chopped
- 1 white radish, peeled, cut in rings
- 1/3 cup gram flour (*besan*) sieved
- 1/4 cup tamarind pulp
- 1/4 cup jaggery
- 1 tsp. chilli powder
- 1/2 tsp. turmeric powder
- 1/3 cup *chana dal*, soaked in water for 2 hours
- 1/2 cup cashewnuts, soaked in water for two hours
- 1/3 cup peanuts, soaked in water for two hours
- 1/3 cup grated *copra*
- 1/2 tsp. saffron
- 1/2 tsp. mustard seeds
- 1/4 tsp. asafoetida
- 1/4 tsp. fenugreek seeds
- 3 tbsp. oil
- Salt to taste

Drain all nuts and *chana dal*. Cook till soft in water. Drain. Reserve. Heat oil in a pressure cooker. Add mustard and fenugreek seeds and asafoetida. Add all leaves and radish, jaggery, powder spices, nuts and dal. Add salt and 3 cups water. Cook under pressure for 7 minutes. Blend. Mix *besan* with a little water smoothly. Add to the vegetable. Add *copra* and simmer till thick and smooth. Serve with *puris*.

Varieties of dals and fluffy puris

Seafood is a speciality in the South.

Bengali ethnic party food

Rajasthani ethnic food includes dry fruit - rice.

Chicken curry :

Festive sweets

METHIYA DAL

(Fenugreek Lentil Curry)

Serves: 6 **Cooking Time: 1 hr**

3/4 cup *tuvar dal*, cooked in 2 cups water
4 *cocum*
3/4 tsp. fenugreek seeds, pounded coarsely
1/3 cup jaggery
1 tsp. *garam masala*
1/2 cup *copra*, synged* and ground
1 tsp. cumin seeds, ground
1/2 tsp. turmeric powder
1 tsp. chilli powder
1/4 tsp. asafoetida
1/2 tsp. mustard seeds
2 cups coriander leaves, chopped
3 tbsp. oil
Salt to taste

Heat oil. Add fenugreek seeds, mustard seeds and asafoetida. Add dal with water, all powder spices, jaggery and salt. Boil till blended, adding water if needed. Add *cocum*, coconut and cumin paste. Simmer and garnish with coriander leaves. Serve with rice.

* lightly brown the *copra* over the gas flame.

PITHI POORI

(Rice Flour Puris)

Serves: 6 **Cooking Time: 1 hr**

$1^1/_2$ cups wholemeal flour (*atta*)
1 cup rice flour
1 tsp. chilli powder
$^1/_4$ tsp. asafoetida
$^1/_2$ tsp. roasted cumin seeds, ground
2 tbsp. ghee
Ghee for frying
Salt to taste

Knead a stiff dough with all ingredients (except ghee for frying) with water. Make equal sized balls. Roll out into 10 to 12 cm discs and fry in batches in hot ghee till puffed up and golden. Serve with any vegetable.

KESARIYA BIRYANI

(Saffron Pulao)

Serves: 6 **Cooking Time: 1 hr**

$1^1/_2$ cup *basmati* rice, soaked in water for 2 hours, drained
8 cloves, pounded
4 pieces cinnamon, pounded
4 cardamoms, pounded
$^1/_2$ cup milk
$^1/_2$ tsp. saffron
1 tsp. cumin seeds
1 tsp. chilli powder
100 gm. cauliflower, chopped
100 gm. peas
2 tomatoes, choppped
1 cup coriander leaves, chopped
$^1/_2$ cup ghee
Salt to taste

Heat ghee in a pressure cooker. Add pounded spices. Brown. Add cumin seeds. Add all vegetables. Stir fry. Add rice and saffron mixed with milk. Add chilli powder and 4 cups hot water. Cook under pressure for 7 minutes. The rice should be fluffy and vegetables cooked. Serve with dal.

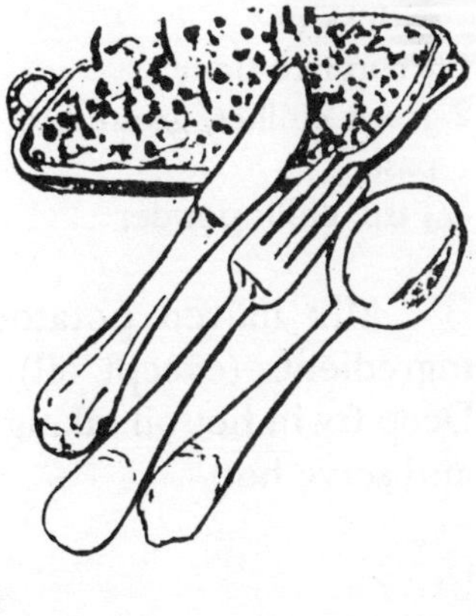

KACHCHE AAM KI CHUTNEY

(Raw Mango Chutney)

Serves: 6 **Cooking Time: 1 hr**

$^1/_2$ kg. grated raw mango
1 lemon-sized ball of jaggery
2 green chillies, minced
1 cup peanuts, roasted, skinned
$^1/_4$ cup coriander leaves, chopped
$^1/_2$ cup grated coconut
Salt to taste

Grind all ingredients coarsely. Serve with the *puja* dinner.

• • •

BHAJA ALOO

(Crisp Baby Potatoes)

Serves: 6 **Cooking Time: 1 hr**

22 small potatoes, boiled with skins
$^1/_2$ cup rice flour
2 green chillies, ground to paste
$^1/_2$ tsp. chilli powder
1 tsp. roasted cumin seed powder
$^1/_4$ tsp. black salt powder
Oil for frying
Salt to taste

Mix halved potatoes with the flour, and all other ingredients (except oil) so the mixture coats each piece. Deep fry in hot oil taking care to separate each piece. Drain and serve hot.

AAM AUR KELE KA RASAYAN

(Mango Banana Sweet)

Serves: 6 **Cooking Time: 30 mins**

4 cups thick coconut milk
1 cup jaggery, melted
1 tsp. cardamom powder
2 mangoes, peeled, chopped
2 bananas, sliced

Melt jaggery fully in cold coconut milk. Add fruit and cardamom powder. Chill before serving. Cubed honeydew melon can also be used but by itself.

MIRCHI POHE USAL

(Flaked Rice)

Servers: 8 **Cooking Time: 1 hr**

$2^1/_2$ cups thick *pohe* (flaked rice), dipped in water for 3 mins,drained
5 red chillies, cut into halves
1 tsp. mustard seeds
2 tsp. sugar
8 curry leaves
2 cups grated coconut
$^1/_2$ cup coconut water
3 tbsp. oil
Salt to taste

Mix drained *pohe* with salt and sugar. Heat oil. Add mustard seeds, curry leaves and chillies. When they pop, add *pohe* and stir till hot and cooked. Sprinkle with coconut water and cook till soft. Serve topped with fresh coconut gratings.

VATANA KARANJIS

(Pea Flipovers)

Serves: 6 **Cooking Time: 1 hr**

2 cups wholemeal flour (*atta*)
1 cup fine semolina
2 tbsp. ghee
Salt to taste

For filling:
$1^1/_2$ cups peas, cooked and mashed slightly
2 green chillies, minced
$^1/_4$ tsp. turmeric powder
1 tsp. sugar
2 tbsp. coconut,ground
$^1/_2$ tsp. cumin seeds
1 tbsp. oil
Salt to taste
Oil for frying

Make a stiff dough of flour, semolina, ghee and salt, adding water. Reserve

Heat 1 tbsp. oil. Add cumin seeds, green chillies. Add peas and all other ingredients. Blend.

Make balls of the dough and equal portions of the filling. Roll out *puri*-like disks and put one portion of stuffing on each. Fold over, press edges and cut with a fluted cutter. Fry *karanjis* in batches in hot oil till golden. Drain and serve with any chutney.

BADAM KI BARFI

(Almond Fudge)

Serves: 6 **Cooking Time: 1 hr 30 mins**

2 cups almonds, soaked in water peeled
2 litres milk, thickened by simmering
2 cups sugar
$^1/_2$ tsp. cardamom powder
2 pieces silver *varkh*

Grind almonds to a paste. Add to milk and cook till dry. Add sugar to $^3/_4$ cup water and boil till a 2 string syrup is obtained. Mix almond paste with the syrup. Pat mixture onto a greased plate. Cool, cover with *varkh* and cut into squares.

• • •

BESAN KI MITHAI

(Gram Flour Sweet)

Serves: 6 **Cooking Time: 1 hr**

500 gm. gram flour (*besan*)
200 gm. ghee
350 gm. ground sugar
1 tsp. cardamom powder

Heat ghee and roast flour in it till pink on a low flame. Add sugar and stir till blended. Pat into a greased *thali* and cool. Cut into squares.

ALOO SAUNF KI PURI

(Potato Puris)

Serves: 6 **Cooking Time: 1 hr**

500 gm. flour (*maida*)
4 large potatoes, boiled, peeled mashed
1/2 cup ground sugar
1/2 tsp. salt
1 tsp. aniseed,pounded finely
1 cup milk
Ghee for frying

Knead all ingredients together (except ghee), adding water to make a firm dough. Make into small balls and roll out 10 cm. discs. Deep fry in hot ghee. Drain well and serve with apple relish.

• • •

SEB KI CHUTNEY

(Apple Relish)

Serves: 6 **Cooking Time: 40 mins**

4 apples, peeled, chopped
1 tsp. lemon juice
1/2 cup sugar, ground
1/4 cup raisins
1 cup vinegar

Mix all ingredients and cook till chutney is solid and browned. Cool and bottle.

RAJALI KELE KI MITHI POLI

(Banana Roti)

Serves: 6 **Cooking Time 1 hr 30 mins**

6 *Rajali* bananas, peeled, chopped
2 cups flour (*maida*)
$^1/_2$ cup sugar
1 tsp. cardamom powder
Ghee as needed
A little oil

Sieve and knead the flour by adding a little oil and water and make into a stiff dough. Reserve.

Cook the bananas on a low fire, adding a little ghee and sugar. Cook till the sugar dissolves and the mixture is solid. Make this filling and the dough into equal number of balls. Roll each dough ball into a small 10 cm. puri. Put one ball of the banana mixture. Close the edges and remake it into a thin *chapati.* Fry on both sides on a greased griddle. Smear ghee on both sides. Serve hot or cold.

AAM KA MITHA

(Mango Cake)

Serves: 6 **Cooking Time: 1 hr 30 mins**

4 cups fresh mango pulp
4 cups sugar
2 cups mawa, ground
1/2 tsp. cardamom powder
1/2 cup ghee
1 tbsp. almonds, sliced
A little milk

Blend the mango pulp in a liquidiser. Heat 2 tsp. ghee in a heavy pan and add the mango pulp and cook on a medium heat. Cook till the mango juice is thick. Leave aside.

In another pan, make a syrup of the sugar. Add a little milk and remove the froth on top. Cook till one thread consistency is obtained. Add the thickened mango juice, ground *mawa* and remaining ghee. Cook till the mixture leaves the sides of the vessel. Add cardamom powder. Pat into a greased plate and leave to cool. While still warm, decorate with sliced almonds and cut into squares.

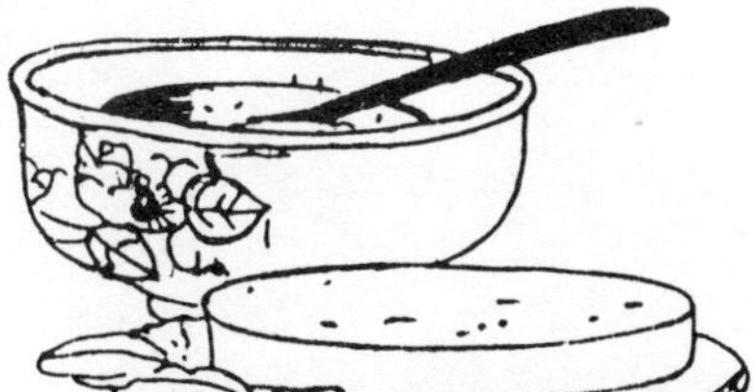

family celebrations

The family in India undoubtedly is a sacrosanct entity. With its spirit of unity and mutual respect, the Indian family has survived the threats posed by technology, materialism, and the thousand other ups and downs which families face everywhere.

One of the bonds which has cemented family ties in India is the numerous celebrations a family holds, bringing together cousins, uncles, aunts, nephews and in-laws. A new arrival, a baby's naming ceremony, a wedding, a festival get-together—these are greeted with spirit and grand celebrations. Though each *Samskara* or sacrament is marked by traditional feasts, here I have chosen to take a more modern look at families eating together. What can busy families do when they have little time to do formal cooking ? They can innovate a fast food party ! What can they do to make a birthday memorable ? They can plan a feast which attracts young and old alike and close the generation gap ! What can they do to enhance the mood of participation ? They can mix and match dishes to create a lovely hodge-podge .

Here are three different family menus. All non-traditional, non-conformist. And by their very nature, they are created for an innovative hostess!

Fast Food at Home

menu–I

dabroti ke patties
dahiwale bhagala noodles
murgh tangri fry
jaldi chini chawal
sabzi ka stew aur pau
kesariya mitha
jardaloo ka suvidh mitha

A Child's Birthday

menu–II

keeme ke hamburgers
badami nankhatai
tilwale toast
nariel ka custard
teen padari roti
khatte mithe aloo
rang birangi cake
jambhare doughnuts

Family Get-together

menu–III

khasta roti
gosht rashida
bajbhatta chawal
machchli khatti pudinewali
lauki ka raita
paneer methiwala
badam ke macroon

DABROTI KE PATTIES

(Bread Patties)

Serves: 6 **Cooking Time: 1 hr**

10 slices of bread
2 cups cooked, chicken shredded
2 slices ham, shredded
2 green chillies, minced
1 tbsp. coriander leaves, chopped
Salt and pepper to taste

To Make sauce:
3 tbsp. flour (*maida*)
2 tbsp. ghee
2 cups milk
Salt and pepper

To fry::
3 eggs, beaten
Oil

To make sauce: Mix flour and ghee and stir fry gently. Add milk, salt and pepper. Beat till no lumps remain. Cool. Add chicken to to the sauce. Add ham,chillies and coriander leaves. Mix well.Cut bread slices into triangles. Pile mixture on each slice and cover with another, getting 10 patties. Dip in beaten egg and deep fry till golden. Serve with tomato sauce.

DAHIWALE BHAGALA NOODLES

(Noodles in Yoghurt)

Serves: 6 **Cooking Time: 30 mins**

2 cups noodles, boiled in salted water, drained
1 capsicum, chopped, seeds removed
1 cucumber, peeled, chopped
1 tomato, chopped
2 green chillies, minced
2 tbsp. coriander leaves, chopped
5 curry leaves
1/2 cup cashew and peanuts, soaked in water for 2 hours peeled
1/2 tsp. mustard seeds
5 cups yoghurt
1 tbsp. oil
Salt and sugar to taste

Mix all ingredients except oil, curry leaves and mustard seeds. Mix well. Heat oil and add mustard seeds. When they pop, add curry leaves. Cool and pour over noodles. Chill and serve cold, adding more yoghurt or milk if mixture is too thick.

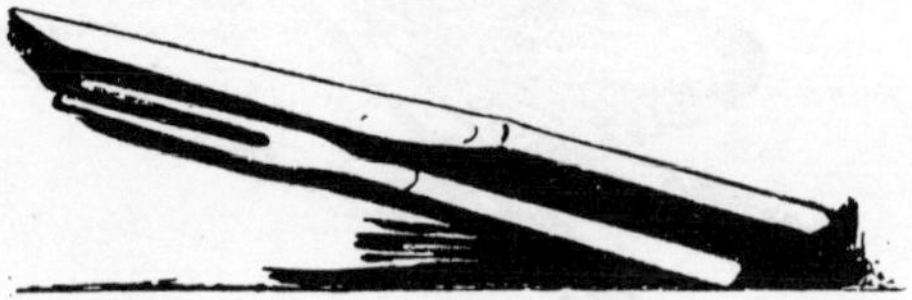

MURGH TANGRI FRY

(Fried Mustard Chicken)

Serves: 6 **Cooking Time: 1 hr**

6 chicken legs, skinned
2 tbsp. flour (*maida*)
1 tsp. mustard powder
1 tsp. pepper powder
1 tsp. chilli powder
3 eggs, beaten
3 cups breadcrumbs
1 tbsp. flour for gravy
1 tbsp. butter
2 tbsp. mayonneise
Oil for frying
Salt to taste

Pressure cook chicken till just done. Wipe chicken pieces. Roll in mustard powder, pepper, chilli and salt and then in flour. Reserve for 5 minutes. Then dip in egg and breadcrumbs. Deep fry till done.

The water in which chicken was cooked may be used to make a gravy with leftover mustard, flour and pepper. In that case, heat butter, gently fry flour mixture and add the soup. Beat till there are no lumps. Cool and add mayonnaise and salt if needed. Serve chicken with this sauce.

JALDI CHINI CHAWAL

(Quick Fried Rice)

Serve: 6 **Cooking Time: 30 mins**

4 cups cooked rice
1 cup mushrooms, chopped
1 cup peas, boiled
1 cup spring onions, chopped
1 egg

4 tbsp. ketchup
2 tbsp. soya sauce
$^1/_2$ tsp. mustard sauce or vinegar
3 tbsp. oil
Salt to taste

Heat oil. Fry onions. Then add mushrooms. Add peas and fry. Add rice. Mix well, adding all sauces and salt. Reserve. Make an omelette using one egg. Beat thoroughly and pour in a greased pan. Cook on both sides. Remove. Cut into strips and mix with rice. Heat and serve.

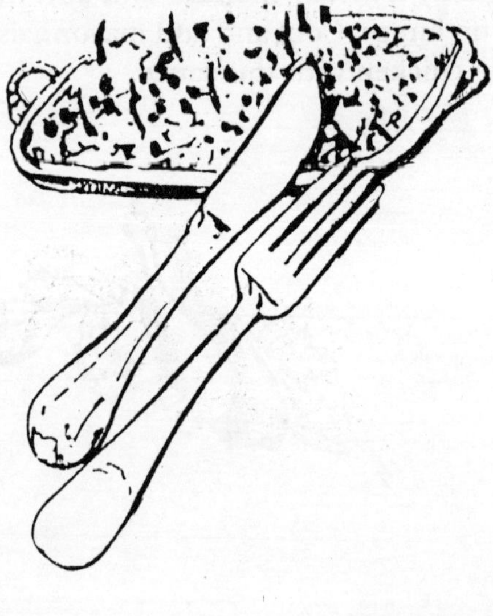

SABZI KA STEW AUR PAU

(Stew and Bread)

Serves: 6 **Cooking Time: 1 hr**

3 tbsp. grated coconut
3 cloves
2 pieces cinnamon
3 tbsp. flour (*maida*)
2 onions, chopped
2 cups peas, boiled
3 potatoes, boiled,peeled cubed
2 tomatoes,cubed
2 tbsp. coriander leaves, chopped
8 *pau* bread cut into havles
3 tbsp. butter
3 tbsp. oil
Salt and sugar to taste

Heat 1 tbsp. oil. Roast coconut, cloves and cinnamon lightly. Grind to a paste. In a little oil, roast the flour till golden. Reserve.

Heat remaining oil and fry onions till golden. Add vegetables and chillies and blend. Add roasted flour mixed smoothly with $^1/_2$ cup water. Stir and add ground paste. Add salt and sugar and coriander leaves. Simmer and reserve. Fry *pau* with butter smeared on each. Serve hot with stew.

KESARIYA MITHA

(Saffron Pudding)

Serves: 6 **Cooking Time: 1 hr**

2 $^3/_4$ cups flour (*maida*)
1$^1/_2$ tsp. baking powder
1$^1/_2$ cups sugar, ground
1$^1/_2$ cups milk
1 cup ghee, melted
$^1/_4$ cup semolina
$^1/_2$ tsp. saffron
Handful of raisins
A pinch of salt

Mix milk and sugar. Add ghee and sifted flour. Beat well. Add semolina and baking powder. Add saffron and salt. Beat well. Grease 12 moulds. Put a few raisins and top with batter. Cook in a steamer till done and a knife pierced comes out clean. Serve with custard sauce.

JARDALOO KA SUVIDH MITHA

(Apricot Quickee)

Serves: 6 **Cooking Time: 45 mins**

$^3/_4$ cup apricots, soaked in water for 2 hours, seeded
6 slices brown bread
1 tbsp. butter
2 eggs, beaten
3 cups milk
$^1/_4$ cup sugar
$^1/_4$ cup *demorara* or brown sugar
1 tsp. vanilla essence

Mash apricots. Reserve. Butter bread. Arrange three slices in a dish. Cover with apricots. Put the remaining three slices over. Beat eggs, sugar and milk. Add vanilla. Pour custard over the bread and bake for 35 minutes or till firm. Sprinkle brown sugar over and serve hot or cold.

KEEME KE HAMBURGERS

(Homemade Hamburgers)

Serves: 6 **Cooking Time: 1 hr 30 mins**

400 gm. minced mutton
2 large potatoes, boiled, peeled, mashed
1 onion, minced
1 tbsp. ginger-garlic paste
1 tsp. chilli powder
1 tsp. garam masala powder
1 tsp. mint leaves, chopped
2 eggs, beaten
1 cup breadcrumbs
6 buns, slit into horizontal halves
2 onions, sliced
2 tomatoes, sliced
12 lettuce leaves
3 tbsp. ketchup
1 tbsp. butter
Oil as needed
Salt and pepper to taste

Heat 3 tbsp. oil. Add minced onion, ginger-garlic paste. Brown. Add mince and all powder masalas. Add mint and coriander leaves and stir fry till mince is cooked and grainy. Cool and mix with mashed potatoes. Season with salt and pepper. Form into 12 cutlets. Dip in beaten egg, then breadcrumbs and deep fry till crisp. Toast bun halves slightly. Butter them and arrange on a platter. Put one cutlet on each over a bed of lettuce, tomato and onion rings. Dot with ketchup and warm in an oven just before serving.

BADAMI NANKHATAI

(Crisp Almond Cookies)

Serves: 6 **Cooking Time: 45 mins**

$1^1/_2$ cup wholemeal flour (*atta*)
$^1/_2$ cup semolina
1 tsp baking powder
1 cup butter or margarine
1 cup ground sugar
1 tsp. nutmeg powder
$^1/_2$ tsp. vanilla essence
2 tbsp. almonds, minced

Beat sugar and butter together. Add baking powder, flour and semolina. Add nutmeg and vanilla. Knead well. Make small balls and flatten them. Decorate with almonds. Arrange in a greased tray and bake in a medium oven (350°) till golden and crips. Cool and serve.

• • •

TILWALE TOAST

(Sesame Toast)

Serves: 6 **Cooking Time: 1 hr**

15 slices bread, cut into halves
2 tbsp. sesame seeds
3 potatoes, boiled, peeled, mashed
2 tsp. ginger-garlic paste
1 green chilli ground
1 tbsp. soya sauce
1 tbsp. ketchup
Oil for frying
Salt to taste

Knead potato and cornflour with chilli ginger, garlic, soya sauce, ketchup and salt. Apply a layer on each slice of bread. Press some sesame seeds on top. Fry in hot oil till golden and serve with tomato sauce.

NARIEL KA CUSTARD

(Coconut Custard)

Serves: 6 **Cooking Time: 1 hr 15 mins**

4 cups thick coconut milk
3 eggs, beaten
$1^1/_2$ cup jaggery
1 tsp. cardamom powder
1 tsp. sugar

Beat coconut milk, jaggery and eggs together. Add cardamom. In a suitable mould, caramelise the sugar. Pour mixture over and bake or steam till set. While baking keep the mould in a tray of water and then in the oven at medium heat. Insert a knitting needle to check if done. The needle should come out clean. Slice, and serve chilled.

• • •

TEEN PADARI ROTI

(Three Layered Rotis)

Serves: 6 **Cooking Time: 1 hr**

4 cups wholemeal flour (*atta*)
4 tbsp. rice flour
1 cup ghee
Salt to taste

Knead a stiff dough with *atta*, water, salt and 1 tsp. ghee. Make into 36 equal balls. Roll out one into a disc. Apply ghee and rice four. Cover with another *roti*. Repeat till each pile has three *rotis* with rice flour and ghee between the layers. Roll each set to make cylindrical shapes. Cut each into 1 cm slices and roll out each slice to a roti. Fry each roti on a griddle smearing ghee on both sides. Serve with sweet sour potatoes.

KHATTE MITHE ALOO

(Sweet Sour Potatoes)

Serves: 6 **Cooking Time: 30 mins**

4 large potatoes, boiled, peeled, cubed
$^1/_4$ cup tamarind pulp
1/3 cup jaggery
1 tsp. chilli powder
4 onions, chopped
1/3 cup oil
Salt to taste

Heat oil. Add onions. Fry till brown. Add potatoes, jaggery and tamarind. Add salt and chilli powder. Cook till sauce is thick. Serve hot with *rotis.*

RANGBIRANGI CAKE

(Ribbon Cake)

Serves: 6 **Cooking Time: 1 hr 30 mins**

3 cups refined flour (*maida*)
1 tsp. baking powder
4 eggs
$^1/_2$ cup butter or margarine
1 tbsp. chocolate powder
1 tsp. vanilla essence
1 drop cochineal colour
$1^1/_2$ cups ground sugar

Cream butter and sugar till fluffy. Add eggs one by one and beat thoroughly. Add flour and fold in with baking powder. Divide into two portions. To one, add chocolate and blend. To the other, add vanilla and a drop of cochineal. Mix well. In a greased 16 cm mould, put blobs of both colours one over another till batters are over. Bake in a medium oven for 30 minutes or till a pierced needle comes out clean. Cool. Turn out on a plate and cut into slices.

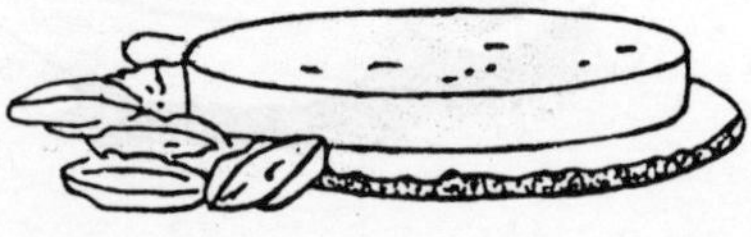

JAMBHARE DOUGHNUTS

(Jam Doughnuts)

Serves: 6 **Cooking Time: 1 hr 30 mins**

3 cups self raising flour (*maida*), sieved
3 tbsp. butter
1 tsp. yeast
1 tbsp. orange rind, grated
2 eggs, beaten
1 egg white
$^1/_2$ cup peach jam
$^1/_2$ cup sugar
1 cup milk
Icing sugar
Oil for frying
$^1/_2$ tsp. salt

Soak yeast in $^1/_2$ cup warm water. Heat butter and milk slowly. Cool slightly. Beat this with yeast. Add sugar, 2 eggs and salt. Add flour and orange rind. Knead well. Leave to rise until double. Knead again. Roll out a thick round and cut with a bowl into 5 cm. rounds. Smear half the rounds with egg white and spoon a little jam on it. Cover with another round and press edges. Complete all. Leave to rise till double. Fry one by one in hot oil. Drain. Sprinkle icing sugar over and cut into halves to serve.

KHASTA ROTI

(Crisp Rotis)

Serves: 8 **Cooking Time: 1 hr**

2 1/2 cups gramflour (*besan*)
1 1/2 cup wholemeal flour (*atta*)
1 tsp. cumin seeds
1/2 cup coriander leaves, chopped
2 green chillis, finely minced
2 tbsp. ghee
Salt to taste

Mix all ingredients and knead a stiff dough with warm water. Make lemon-sized balls and roll out each to 12 cm discs. Cook on a greased griddle till crisp. Serve with green chutney.

GOSHT RASHIDA

(Mutton Rashida)

Serves: 6 **Cooking Time: 1 hr 30 mins**

750 gm. mutton, boneless cubes
2 large onions, grated
1 tbsp. ginger-garlic paste
1 tbsp. coriander-cumin powder
3 tsp. chilli powder
$^{3}/_{4}$ tsp. turmeric powder
1 tbsp. garam masala powder
2 cups yoghurt
2 tomatoes, chopped
6 cloves
6 peppercorns
6 cardamom
2 bay leaves
2 cup oil
1 cup coriander leaves, chopped
Salt to taste

Heat oil in a pressure cooker. Add pepper, cloves, cardamom and bay leaves. Add onion. Fry. Add ginger-garlic paste. Brown. Addtomatoes and all powder spices. Cook till blended. Add yoghurt. Cook till oil separates. Reserve. Heat 3 tbsp. oil in another pan and stir fry meat with enough salt till well browned. Add meat to yoghurt gravy. Add two cups hot water and salt if needed. Cook under pressure for 15 to 20 minutes. Garnish with coriander leaves.

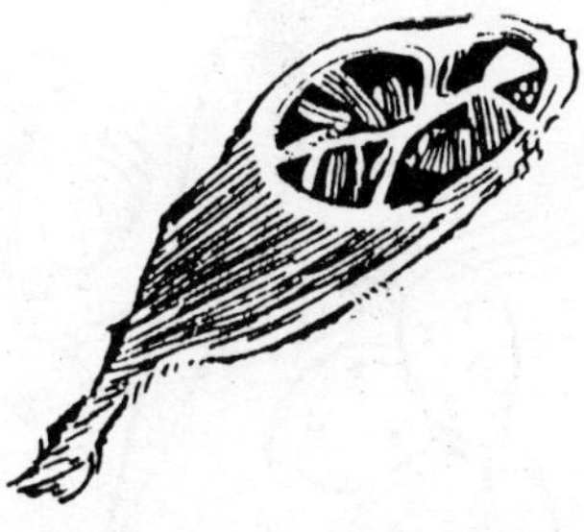

BAJBHATTA CHAWAL

(Mixed Vegetable Pulao)

Serves: 6 **Cooking Time: 1 hr**

2 cups mixed vegetables-cauliflower,peas,potato, green gram etc.
$1^1/_2$ cup *basmati* rice, soaked in water for 2 hours
1 tsp. garam masala powder
1 tsp. chilli powder
$^1/_2$ tsp. turmeric powder
6 cloves
6 cardamoms
1 tbsp. jaggery
$^1/_4$ tsp. asafoetida
5 curry leaves
5 tbsp. oil
Salt to taste

Prepare all vegetables and wash them. Drain rice. In a pressure cooker, heat jaggery and asafoetida. When it melts, add oil. Add cloves and cardamoms and curry leaves. Add vegetables. Stir fry. Add rice and all other spices. Stir till shiny. Add 5 cups hot water and salt. Cook under pressure for 7 minutes or till done and fluffy.

MACHCHLI KHATTI PUDINEWALI

(Sour Fish Curry)

Serves: 6

Cooking Time: 1 hr

12 pieces of pomfret,filleted
$^1/_2$ tsp. turmeric powder
1 tsp. ginger paste
Oil for frying
Salt to taste

Grind to paste:
1 tsp. cumin seed powder
1 tsp. coriander seeds,powder
1 tsp. *amchur*
$^1/_4$ tsp. asafoetida
$^1/_2$ cup coriander leaves, chopped
1 tbsp. mint leaves, chopped

Smear fish with turmeric and salt and deep fry till golden. Drain. Reserve. Heat 2 tbsp. oil from the remaining oil and put in all powder masalas, coriander and mint leaves and salt if needed. Add a little water—$^1/_2$ cup—and when the gravy is smooth, add fish, taking care not to break it. Serve hot with rice.

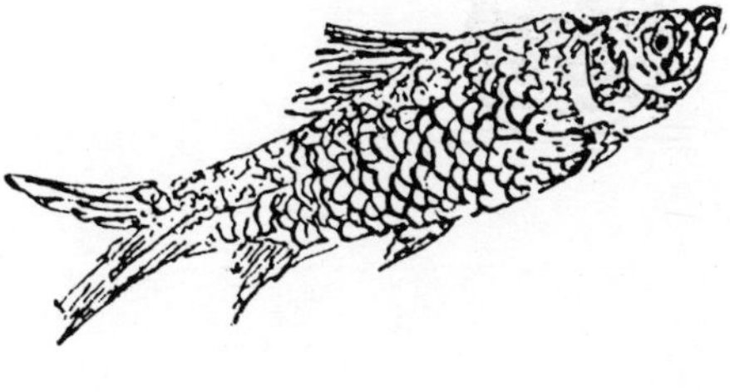

LAUKI KA RAITA

(Bottlegourd Salad)

Servers: 6 **Cooking Time: 45 mins**

2 cups grated bottlegourd cooked, all water removed
$^1/_2$ cup savoury *boondis*
4 cups yoghurt, beaten
1 tsp. roasted cumin seed, powdered
1 tsp. chilli powder
$^1/_2$ tsp. mustard, ground
Salt to taste

Squeeze out all water from the cooked *lauki*. Mix *lauki* with yoghurt Add *boondi* and mix well. Add salt and mustard paste. Place in a bowl. Sprinkle cumin and chilli powder on top and chill.

PANEER METHIWALA

(Paneer with Fenugreek)

Servers: 6 **Cooking Time: 1 hr**

200 gm. *paneer*, cubed
2 bunches *methi*, leaves chosen
2 tsp. *dhana-jeera* powder
1 tsp. chilli powder
$^1/_2$ tsp. turmeric powder
$^1/_4$ tsp. asafoetida
$1^1/_2$ tsp. sugar
1 tsp. garam masala powder
Oil as needed
Salt to taste

Heat oil and fry *paneer* pieces till golden. Put in water for 10 minutes. Drain. Reserve. Heat 4 tbsp. oil from the remaining and add *methi* leaves. Cook till fried well. Add all spices, sugar and lastly the *paneer* and salt. Stir cook for a few minutes. Serve hot.

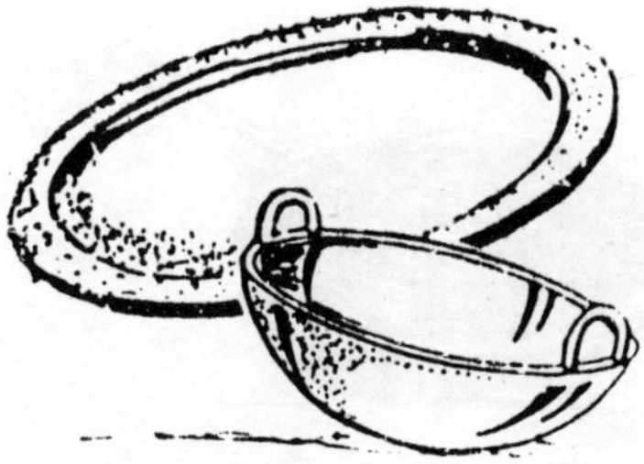

BADAM KE MACROON

(Almond Macroons)

Serves: 6 **Cooking Time: 1 hr**

4 egg whites, beaten stiffly
8 tbsp. rice powder
1/2 tsp. almond essence
2 1/2 cups almond powder
2 1/2 cups ground sugar
1 1/2 cups whipped sweetened cream

Mix almond powder, rice powder and sugar. Put in essence. Gently mix egg whites and make a thick batter. Line a large baking tray with a greased greaseproof paper. Put small blobs of mixture on it and bake in a preheated hot oven for 15 to 20 minutes. Remove. Cool and serve with whipped cream.

women's parties

There's a special air about women getting together. On these relaxed mornings or afternoons they are in their own element and can really entertain their close friends or associates with food which is unusual and menus which are put together with originality. In this category I have included a *chaat* party, for women are reputed to like sweet, sour and pungent dishes. And what's more *chaat* requires less arduous cooking ! So there's more time for cosy chats and to catch up with each other's activities.

A high tea also suits women, for its timing allows them to take a break in a busy schedule and yet reach home when the family needs them. A high tea is a fairly new concept in entertaining and as always, women have taken to it—particularly because most women find this kind of entertaining more suitable than giving a cocktail party.

Two other interesting menus are included here. A salad party is welcome on sweltering summer days or working days when the palate seeks cool and light food. A hotpot party, as its name indicates, is a hot and sour mixture of food from many countries, designed to cater to our taste. In fact, this menu breaks all rules and hence succeeds in being a brilliant hospitality idea. It accommodates last minute changes and a mixture of flavours which is at once titillating and inviting !

Salad Party

menu–I

ananas paneer ka salad
aloo sirke ka salad
navrattan salad
ande aur cheese ka pie
bhune baingan ka salad
barfila dahi falonwala

Kitty Party

menu–II

gosht ke satay kabab
puri masaleki
subzi kurma
chandnooma samose
lal chutney
falon ki chaat
baide ka mitha
chawal ki baked kheer

Chaat Party

menu–III

Moonghfali rassedar aur bhature
mewe ki tikiya
tamatar ki guriya chutney
aloo ki bhooni chaat
kathol ki milijuli chaat
aloo pyaz ke pohe
tamater ka thanda shorba
kalingad ka sharbat
elaichi kulfi

Hot Pot Party

menu–IV

rajama michanwala keema
chawal aur kheeme ka moussaka
makai patties tamatar ke rassewale
sabzi chow chow aur puris
aloo ka sukka aur roti
machhi tamater
khasta biscuit pudding

ANANAS PANEER KA SALAD

(Pineapple Paneer Moulds)

Serves: 6 **Cooking Time: 30 mins**

6 rings of pineapple from a tin
2 cups syrup from the tin
$^1/_4$ cup lemon juice
1 cup *paneer* shreds
1 lettuce, shredded
15 gm. gelatin
1 tbsp. coriander leaves
6 wedges of lemon

Dissolve gelatine in $^1/_2$ cup water. Cool. Add to lemon juice and pineapple syrup. Pour into six moulds and chill till set. In a serving platter, spread lettuce shreds. Arrange six pineapple rings on this. Put the *paneer* shreds in the centre. Unmould each pineapple mould over each pile and decorate with coriander leaves.

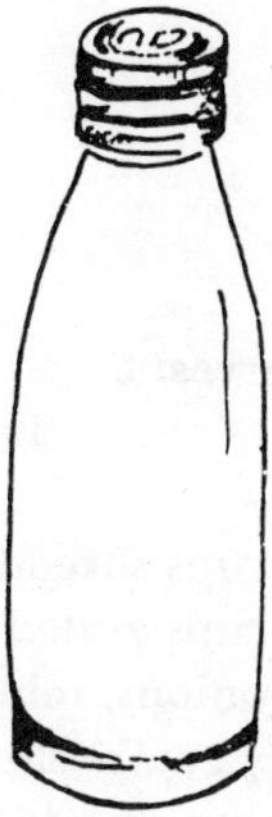

ALOO SIRKE KA SALAD

(Potatoes in Vinegar)

Serves: 6 **Cooking Time: 1 hr 30 mins**

6 potatoes, boiled, peeled, sliced
3 spring onions, chopped
3 sprigs fresh garlic, chopped
1/2 tsp. grated ginger
2 tbsp. vinegar
1 cup shredded cheese
1/2 cup coriander leaves, chopped
3 tbsp. oil
Salt, pepper, sugar to taste

Heat oil. Add onions, garlic and ginger. Add vinegar and salt, sugar and pepper. Mix with potatoes. Cool and add coriander leaves. Arrange on a platter and cover with cheese.

• • •

NAVRATTAN SALAD

(Vegetable and Cheese Salad)

Serves: 6 **Cooking Time: 30 mins**

3 cups shredded cabbage
2 cups grated carrots
2 onions, minced
1/2 cup raisins, washed
2 cup shredded cheese
1 tbsp. vinegar
1 tbsp. lemon juice
1 tbsp. oil
Salt and pepper to taste

Toss all vegetables together and add all seasonings. Cover with cheese and chill before serving.

ANDE AUR CHEESE KA PIE

(Cheese and Egg Pie)

Serves: 6 **Cooking Time: 1 hr 30 mins**

2 cups flour (*maida*), sieved
3/4 cup butter or fat
2 1/2 cups grated cheese
3 eggs, beaten
1 cup soft cooked corn
1/2 cup milk
1/4 tsp. salt
Salt and pepper to taste

Make a stiff dough with flour, salt and fat, adding cold water. Roll out into two rounds of 15 cm each. Put one in a pie dish. Mix eggs, milk and cheese with salt and pepper. Add corn and pour on the pastry. Cover with the other pastry round and join edges with a little milk. Brush top with a little milk and bake in a medium oven for 40 minutes, lowering heat after about 25 minutes. Cook till a needle or fork pierced in comes out clean. Cool and serve slices with salads.

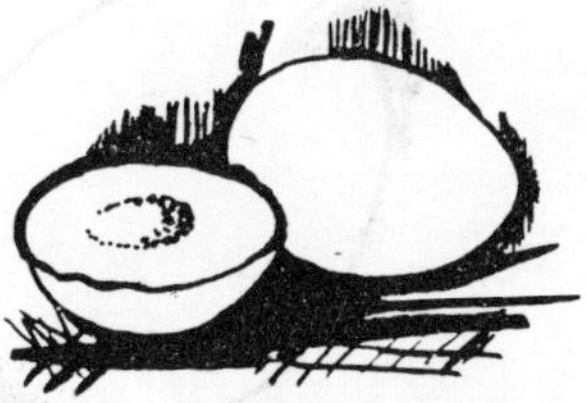

BHUNE BAINGAN KA SALAD

(Baked Brinjals)

Serves: 6 **Cooking Time: 1 hr 30 mins**

3 long, large brinjals
2 tbsp. butter
$1^1/_2$ cup cream
1 cup soft cooked corn
1 cup cooked shredded chicken
$^1/_4$ cup tomato sauce
Salt and pepper

Cut brinjals lengthwise into two. Sprinkle with salt and reserve for 10 minutes. Bake till soft but whole. Remove flesh and cool cases. Mix flesh with cream, chicken, corn, salt and pepper. Pile over the six halves of brinjals. Dot with sauce and serve cold.

BARFILA DAHI FALONWALA

(Fruit Yoghurt)

Serves: 6 **Cooking Time: 1 hr 30 mins**

1 litre milk
2 tbsp. yoghurt
$^1/_2$ tsp. vanilla essence
2 pears,peeled,chopped, sprinkled with lemon juice
1 apple, peeled, chopped, sprinkled with lemon juice
Sugar to taste

Heat milk and thicken to till $^3/_4$ its quantity. Cool. When lukewarm, add sugar, yoghurt and vanilla essence. Arrange chopped fruit in a bowl and pour cooled yoghurt mixture over. Leave to set in a warm place for 6 to 8 hours. When set, chill till needed. Serve very cold, with a sprinkling of finely crushed ice all over.

GOSHT KE SATAY KABAB

(Meat Kababs with Satay Sauce)

Serves: 6 **Cooking Time:1 hr 30 mins**

600 gm. boneless mutton, cubed
3 tbsp. soya sauce
$1^1/_2$ tsp. honey
1 tsp. red chilli paste
1 tsp. *garam masala* powder
1 tbsp. oil
Salt to taste

For Satay Sauce:
2 onions, peeled, grated
1 tsp. garlic paste
1 tsp. chilli powder
1 tsp. *garam masala* powder
1 tsp. ginger paste
$1^1/_2$ cup peanuts, roasted, powdered
$^1/_2$ cup vinegar
2 tbsp. sugar
2 tbsp. jam
Oil as needed
Salt to taste

Mix all ingredients (except sauce) with meat and reserve for 4 hours. Skewer meat pieces on bamboo sticks or skewers and grill until tender.

To make sauce: Heat 3 tbsp. oil. Fry onions, garlic and ginger. Add all other ingredients and cook till blended, adding $^1/_2$ to 1 cup of water as needed. Serve the *kababs* hot with this sauce and onion rings.

PURI MASALEKI

(Masala Puris)

Serves: 6 **Cooking Time: 1 hr**

3 cup wholemeal flour (*atta*) sieved
1/2 cup fine semolina
2 tbsp. coriander leaves, chopped
1/2 tsp. chilli powder
1/2 tsp. *garam masala* powder
Oil as needed
Salt to taste

Knead a stiff dough with the flour and all other ingredients. Add 2 tbsp. hot oil and just enough water to make a smooth dough. Make small marble-sized balls and roll out *puris.* Fry in batches in hot oil. The *puris* should be crisp and puffed up. Drain on to kitchen paper and serve hot with *kurma.*

SUBZI KORMA

(Vegetable Korma)

Serves: 6 **Cooking Time: 1 hr**

8 cauliflower pieces
1 cup peas
2 potatoes, peeled,cubed
1 carrot, peeled, cubed
1 tomatoes, chopped
2 onions, grated
1 tbsp. ginger-garlic paste
1 tsp. chilli powder
1 tbsp. *garam masala* powder
$^1/_2$ tsp. turmeric powder
1 cup coriander leaves, chopped
1 tsp. cumin seeds
4 tbsp. oil
Salt and sugar to taste

Wash all vegetables. Drain. Heat oil. Add cumin seeds. Add onion. Brown. Add ginger-garlic and fry. Add all powder masalas and vegetables. Add salt and sugar. Stir fry till crisp. Then add 2 cups hot water and cook till done. Add coriander leaves and serve with *puris*.

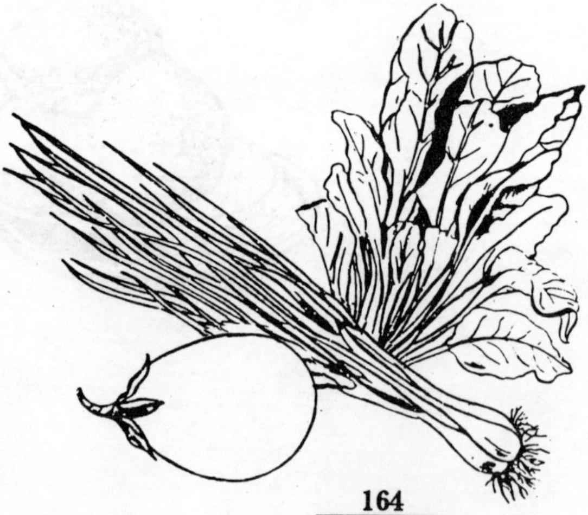

CHANDNOOMA SAMOSA

(Moon Samosas)

Serves: 6 **Cooking Time: 1 hr**

3 cups plain flour (*maida*)
2 tbsp. ghee
A pinch of soda bicarb
Oil as needed
Salt to taste

For the filling:
500 gm. minced mutton
1 tsp. ginger-garlic paste
1 onion, grated
1 tsp. chilli powder
$^1/_2$ tsp. turmeric powder
1 tsp. garam masala powder
1 tsp. sugar
$^1/_2$ cup coriander leaves
$^1/_2$ cup green peas, cooked
Oil as needed
Salt to taste

Heat 3 tbsp. oil. Add onion. Brown. Add ginger-garlic paste. Brown. Add mince and all powder masalas. Stir fry till grainy. Add one cup water and cook till done and dry. Add peas, salt and sugar and blend well.

Knead a stiff dough with flour, ghee, soda bicarb and salt. Make lemon-sized balls. Roll out each to 10 cm. diameter. Put a spoonful of filling in the centre. Fold over and close the edges, fluting the ends. Make all *samosas.*

Keep oil in a pan for deep frying. Fry in batches of 3 to 4 till golden. Drain on kitchen paper and serve with chutney.

LAL CHUTNEY

(Red Chutney)

Serves: 6 **Cooking Time: 45 mins**

1 cup grated fresh coconut
3 red chillies
1/2 tsp. garlic paste
1 tsp. tamarind paste
Salt to taste

Grind all ingredients till they are blended into a fine chutney.

• • •

FALON KI CHAAT

(Fruit Savoury)

Serves: 6 **Cooking Time: 30 mins**

1 orange, peeled, segmented
1 apple, peeled, cubed
1 pear, peeled, cubed
2 bananas, sliced
1/2 pineapple, cubed
1/2 tsp. rock salt
1 tsp. cumin seeds
1 tbsp. lemon juice
1 tbsp. mint leaves, chopped
Salt to taste

Mix all fruit, salt, rock salt, lemon juice and mint leaves in a bowl. Dry-roast cumin seeds. Pound to a coarse powder. Sprinkle over fruit and chill before serving.

BAIDE KA MITHA

(Custard Tart)

Serves: 6 **Cooking Time:1 hr 30 mins**

For shell:
$1^1/_2$ cups flour (maida)
$^1/_4$ tsp. baking powder
1 egg, beaten lightly
$^1/_3$ cup sugar, ground
$^1/_2$ cup butter
A pinch of salt

For filling:
3 eggs
1 tsp. vanilla essence
2 cups milk or
$^1/_2$ tin condensed milk
Ground sugar to taste
1 tsp. nutmeg powder

For shell:

Whisk butter and sugar till creamy. Add salt. Add egg gradually and beat continuously. Add sieved flour and baking powder and knead till dough resembles breadcrumbs. Add water and knead till smooth. Chill for $^1/_2$ hr . Roll out into a large disc and cover a 24 cm. pie dish without breaking pastry. Pat down edges and decorate them by using a spoon or fork to make markings. Brush with egg white and reserve.

For filling:

Beat eggs and sugar till smooth. Add vanilla. Heat milk gently. If condensed milk is used, make upto 2 cups and do not add sugar unless needed. Add egg to milk and stir till creamy. Spoon the custard into the pie shell without spilling. Bake in a medium oven for 45 minutes or till done and custard is firm. Cool. Sprinkle nutmeg powder over and cut into slices to serve.

CHAWAL KI BAKED KHEER

(Rice Pudding)

Serves: 6 **Cooking Time: 1 hr**

$^1/_2$ cup coarse rice granules
2 cups milk
3 eggs, beaten
2 tbsp. mixed nuts, chopped
1 tsp. vanilla essence
1 tbsp. raisins
One pinch saffron
Castor sugar to taste

Boil or cook rice flour in 2 cups water and drain away excess water. Mix eggs, vanilla and sugar and add nuts and raisins. Add cooked rice granules. Add milk and mix well. Put in a baking dish and bake in a medium oven for 40 minutes or till done. The top should be golden and crisp.

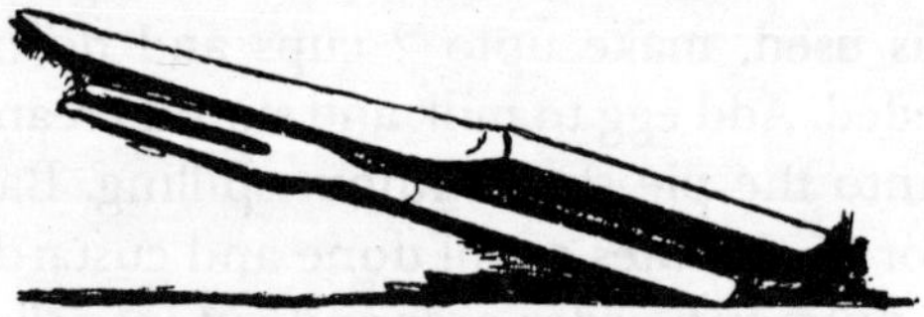

MOONGFALI RASSEDAR AUR BHATURE

(Peanut Curry with Puffed Puris)

Serves: 6 **Cooking Time: 1 hr 30 mins**

2 cups unroasted peanuts, soaked in water for 4 hours
2 green chillies
2 potatoes, peeled,cubed
2 tomatoes, minced
2 onions, minced
1 tbsp. ginger-garlic paste
1 tsp. garam masala powder
1 tsp. chilli powder
$^1/_2$ tsp. turmeric powder
1 tsp. *amchur* powder
1 tsp. *anardana*, ground
2 green chillies
1 cup coriander leaves, chopped
1 lemon, cut into wedges
4 tbsp. oil
Salt and sugar to taste

Cook peanuts till soft and reserve. Heat oil. Add onion, ginger and garlic. Brown. Add tomatoes. Blend. Add all powder masalas and potatoes. Stir fry till masala coats the potatoes. Add a little water and salt and cook till soft. Add cooked peanuts, more salt if needed and sugar as per taste. Simmer till blended. Serve garnished with fried green chillies, coriander leaves and lemon wedges.

BHATURE

(White Puris)

Serves: 6 **Cooking Time: 1 hr**

3 cup self raising flour (*maida*)
$^1/_2$ cup yoghurt
Oil for frying
Salt to taste

Mix flour, yoghurt and salt and knead a stiff dough with water. Leave for 1 hr.. Then make small balls and roll out each to 9 cm. discs. Deep fry in hot oil till puffed up. Serve with *Rassedar Moongfali.*

MEWE KI TIKIYA

(Dry Fruit Cutlets)

Serves: 6 **Cooking Time: 1 hr**

5 potatoes, boiled, peeled, mashed
5 tsp. arrowroot powder
1 tsp. cumin seeds, roasted powdered
$1^1/_2$ cup mixed almonds, cashewnuts
$^1/_2$ tsp. green chilli paste
$^1/_2$ tsp. ginger paste
$^1/_2$ tsp. *amchur* powder
$^1/_2$ garam masala powder
$^1/_2$ tsp. sugar
Oil for frying
Salt to taste raisins chopped finely

Mash potatoes and leaving 2 tbsp. mash, mix with the arrowroot leaving 2 tbsp. Add cumin seed powder and salt to taste. Knead into a stiff dough.

Mix all nuts, chilli/ginger paste, sugar, salt and all masalas with 2 tbsp. mashed potatoes.

Make small flat discs of potato dough. Place small portion of the stuffing on it and fold to cover all around. Sprinkle each tiki with a little arrowroot and water mixture and deep fry till golden.

TAMATAR KI GURIYA CHUTNEY

(Tomato Chutney)

Serves: 6 **Cooking Time: 15 mins**

3 tomatoes, minced
2 green chillies, minced
$1^1/_2$ tsp. jaggery
$^1/_2$ tsp. cumin/fenugreek seeds
1 tbsp. coriander leaves, minced
2 tsp. oil
Salt to taste

Heat oil. Add cumin and fenugreek seeds. Add green chillies and tomatoes. Add jaggery and salt. Cook till mashed and blended. Add coriander leaves and serve with *tikiyas.*

ALOO KI BHOONI CHAAT

(Potato Savoury)

Serves: 6 **Cooking Time: 1 hr**

6 large potatoes, boiled, peeled, finely cubed
3 green chillies, minced
1 tsp. cumin seeds
4 cups yoghurt, beaten
$^1/_2$ cup raisins, washed
1 tsp. roasted cumin seed powder
$^1/_2$ tsp. chilli powder
$^1/_2$ cup tamarind-jaggery chutney
$^1/_2$ cup coriander-mint leaves, minced
1 tomato, finely sliced
3 tbsp. oil
Salt and *chaat masala* to taste

Heat oil. Add cumin seeds and green chillies. Add potatoes. Stir fry till fragrant. Add salt. Cool thoroughly. Put in a serving dish. Pour salted yoghurt over. Sprinkle raisins, roasted cumin seed powder, chilli powder, coriander and mint leaves and *chaat masala.* Sprinkle chutney also. Decorate with tomato slices. Chill and serve.

Note: Make tamarind-jaggery chutney by cooking $^1/_2$ cup jaggery and $^1/_2$ cup tamarind pulp with salt and a little chilli powder till blended. Cool.

KATHOL KI MILIJULI CHAAT

(Mixed Pulses)

Serves: 6 **Cooking Time: 1 hr**

1 cup sprouted *red chanas*, cooked
1 cup sprouted *moong*, cooked
2 potatoes, boiled, peeled, cubed
1/2 cup savoury *boondis*
1 cup tamarind jaggery chutney
5 cups yoghurt, beaten
2 green chillies, minced
1 tsp. chilli powder
1 tsp. cumin seeds, roasted powdered
1 cup croutons, finely cut bread, fried till crisp
Salt and sugar to taste

Mix sprouted beans, potatoes with yoghurt, green chillies salt and sugar. Put in a bowl and chill. Sprinkle chilli powder, cumin seed powder, chutney, coriander leaves and croutons. Add savoury boondis just before serving.

ALOO PYAZ KE POHE

(Flaked Rice Savoury)

Serves: 6 **Cooking Time: 1 hr**

2 cup flaked rice, thick variety (dip in water for 3 minutes, drain and spread on a piece of cloth)
1 cup green peas, cooked
1 potato, boiled, peeled, diced
2 onions, finely chopped
3 green chillies,minced
$^1/_2$ tsp. turmeric powder
2 cups grated coconut
1 cup coriander leaves, chopped
1 tsp. mustard/cumin seeds
8 curry leaves
2 tsp. sugar
1 lemon, cut into wedges
5 tbsp. oil
Salt to taste

Heat oil. Add mustard and cumin seeds. When they pop, add onion green chillies and curry leaves. Brown. Add peas and potatoes. Add turmeric and salt to taste. Blend. Add moist *pohe* and sprinkle with water from time to time, add salt if needed and sugar and stir to mix well. When done, put in a bowl. Sprinkle coconut and coriander leaves over and serve with lemon pieces.

TAMATER KA THANDA SHORBA

(Tomato Cocktail)

Serves: 6 **Cooking Time: 30 mins**

5 tomatoes, skinned, tough pith removed
2 tsp. pepper sauce or chilli sauce
4 tsp. sugar
2 tsp. lemon juice
2 tbsp. small pieces of tomato
2 tbsp. mint leaves, chopped
Salt to taste

Liquidise tomatoes till fine. Remove any hard threads or pieces. Add salt, pepper, chilli sauce, sugar, lemon juice and whisk well. Pour into glasses and top with mint leaves and tomato pieces. Chill and serve.

• • •

KALINGAD KA SHARBAT

(Watermelon Sherbet)

Serves 6: **Cooking Time: 30 mins**

5 cups watermelon flesh, seeded
1/2 tsp. vanilla essence
1/2 cup sweetened cream
Sugar to taste

Liquidise everything except cream. Put into glasses. Chill. Top with a little cream before serving.

ELAICHI KULFI

(Cardamom Ice-cream)

Serves: 6 **Cooking Time: 1 hr 30 mins**

$1^1/_2$ litre milk
1 cup *khoya*, ground
1 tsp cardamom essence
3 tbsp. custard powder
A pinch of cardamom powder
Sugar to taste

Heat milk. Add sugar and *khoya* and beat with an eggbeater till blended.

Mix custard powder with a little milk smoothly and cook till done. Cool. Add to the cooled milk mixture. Whisk and add cardamom essence and powder. Blend. Fill into *kulfi* moulds and seal tops with dough. Freeze till ready and serve with cream (optional).

RAJMA MIRCHANWALA KEEMA

(Chilli Con Carne)

Serves: 6 **Cooking Time: 1 hr**

500 gm. minced mutton (*kheema*) cooked
200 gm. *rajma* beans, soaked in water overnight, cooked
2 cups tomato *puree*
3 onions, grated
1/2 cup oil
2 tsp. chilli powder
1 tsp. pepper powder
1/2 tsp. *oregano*
1/2 tsp. garlic paste
Salt and pepper to taste

Heat oil in a pressure cooker. Add onions and garlic. Brown. Add tomato *puree*. Brown. Add mince, salt, sugar, *oregano*, chilli and pepper powders. Simmer after first whistle for few minutes. Serve with crusty bread.

CHAWAL AUR KEEME KA MOUSSAKA

(Rice Moussaka)

Serves: 6 **Cooking Time: 1 hr**

4 cups cooked rice
2 cups minced mutton, cooked
3 cup tomato *puree*
$1^1/_2$ cup grated onion
1 tbsp. ginger-garlic paste
2 tsp. chilli powder
1 tsp. cumin seed powder
10 slices of brinjal, fried
2 cups grated cheese
$^1/_2$ cup butter
Salt and pepper to taste

Heat butter. Fry onion and ginger-garlic paste. Add tomato *puree.* Fry till blended. Add mince. Fry. Add rice and mix. Add chilli and cumin powders, salt and pepper. Put into a greased dish. Cover with fried brinjals and cheese. Dot with butter and heat in the oven before serving.

MAKAI PATTIES TAMATAR KE RASSEWALE

(Corn Patties in Tomato Sauce)

Serves: 6 **Cooking Time: 1 hr 30 mins**

2 cups corn kernels,cooked soft
2 green chillies, minced
1 onion chopped or grated, fried
1 tbsp. coriander leaves
1 tsp. cumin powder
6 potatoes, boiled, peeled, mashed
3 slices bread
Oil for frying
Salt to taste

3 cups tomato *puree*
3 cups spring onions, chopped
1 tbsp. ginger-garlic paste
$^1/_2$ cup ketchup
1 tsp. chilli powder
$^1/_3$ cup oil
Salt and sugar to taste

Mix corn, green chillies, coriander, cumin powder and grated onion. Knead mashed potatoes with wet bread and salt. Make 12 balls. Flatten each and put a portion of corn in it. Bind all round. Prepare all patties and fry in hot oil till golden. Reserve.

Heat $^1/_3$ cup oil. Add spring onions, ginger-garlic paste. Brown. Add tomato *puree*. Brown. Add chilli powder, ketchup, salt and sugar. Blend. Arrange patties in a dish and pour sauce over. Serve hot.

SABZI CHOW CHOW AUR PURIS

(Vegetable Chow Chow with Puris)

Serves: 6 **Cooking Time: 1 hr**

200 gm. carrots, peeled, chopped
200 gm. french beans
2 potatoes, boiled, peeled, cubed
2 capsicums, chopped
1 tsp. chilli powder
1 tsp. mustard seeds
1 tsp. fenugreek seeds
$^1/_2$ cup peanuts/cashewnuts, cooked
1 tbsp. lemon juice
$^1/_4$ tsp. asafoetida
4 tbsp. oil
Salt to taste

In one tsp. hot oil, fry mustard, fenugreek and asafoetida. Grind with chilli powder. Reserve.

Heat remaining oil. Fry chopped vegetables till nearly done. Add nuts and potatoes. Add salt and ground paste. Add lemon juice and a little sugar if wanted. Serve cold or hot with *puris.*

ALOO KA SUKKA AUR ROTI

(Potatoes with Roti)

Serves: 6 **Cooking Time: 1 hr**

4 potatoes, boiled, peeled chopped
1 cup coconut grated
1 tbsp. tamarind pulp
1/2 tsp. turmeric powder
4 red chillies
1 tbsp. coriander seeds
2 cloves
1 tsp. black gram (*urad*) dal
4 tbsp. oil
1/2 tsp. mustard seeds
5 curry leaves
Salt and sugar to taste

In one tsp. oil, fry coriander seeds, cloves, *urad* dal and red chillies. Grind with coconut, tamarind and turmeric to a paste.

Heat remaining oil. Add mustard seeds and curry leaves. When they pop, add potatoes and the paste. Add salt and sugar. Simmer once. Serve with *rotis.*

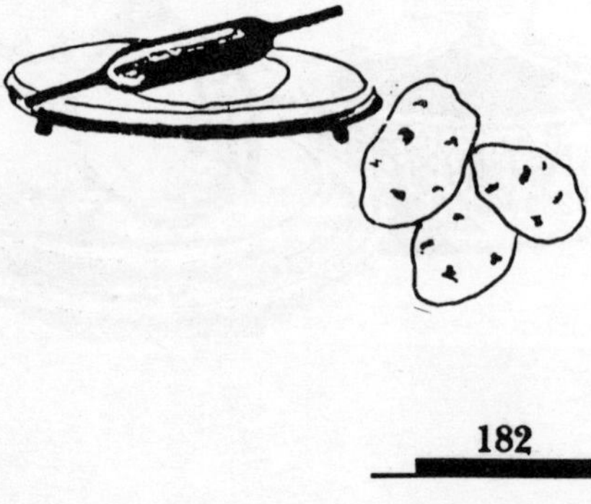

MACHHI TAMATER

(Tomato Fish)

Serves: 6 **Cooking Time: 1 hr**

2 pomfrets, boned, filleted
1 tbsp. lemon juice
1 tbsp. flour
3 cup tomato *puree*
1 tsp. ginger-garlic paste
1 cup spring onion, minced
1 tbsp. coriander leaves
$^1/_2$ cup ketchup
1 tsp. chilli powder
1 green chilli minced
Oil for frying
Salt to taste

Apply lemon juice, salt and flour to fish. Fry in 1 cup hot oil. Drain. Reserve. In the same oil, add spring onion, ginger and garlic. Brown. Add tomato *puree*, ketchup and chilli powder. Cook till oil separates. Add salt and fish pieces. Heat and garnish with green chilli pieces. Serve with bread.

KHASTA BISCUIT PUDDING

(Crisp Pudding)

Serves: 6 **Cooking Time: 1 hr**

3 cups custard
6 crunchy cookies(biscuits)
$^1/_2$ cup walnut kernels
2 cup mixed chopped fruit
2 cups double cream
$^1/_2$ cup ground sugar
1 tsp. vanilla essence
3 cherries.

In a dish, put a layer of eight broken cookies. Put half a layer of the fruit and then half a layer of the custard. Repeat. Top with whipped cream made with cream, sugar and vanilla. Decorate with sliced cherries. Chill and serve.

Note: To make custard, mix $1^1/_2$ tbsp. custard powder with 3 cups milk smoothly. Add $^3/_4$ cup sugar and $^1/_2$ tsp. vanilla essence. Cook till creamy and smooth. Cool and use.